CW01661300

H[illegible]

SIMPL[illegible]CTIVE

# CONSULTANT APPOINTMENTS

IN JUST

# 500

WORDS

Enjoy

To my husband Brian who supports me to achieve my goals, celebrates my successes with panache, and provides wise and balanced advice (but only when asked) – much like this book is intended to help you.

# HOW TO WRITE SIMPLE AND EFFECTIVE CONSULTANT APPOINTMENTS IN JUST 500 WORDS

SARAH FOX

500
WORDS

Copyright © 2017– Sarah Jane Victoria Fox

First published in Great Britain in 2017

Published by
500 Words Ltd
Ash Cottage
Hawthorn Lane
Wilmslow
Cheshire
SK9 5DG

All rights reserved. No part of this publication may be reproduced, stored in a retrieval system or transmitted in any form or by any means without prior written permission, nor be otherwise circulated in any form of binding or cover other than that in which it is published and without a similar condition being imposed on the subsequent purchaser.

A catalogue record for this book is available from the British Library.

ISBN: 978-0-9955409-1-0

Book design and typesetting by Ashdown Creative
www.ashdowncreative.co.uk

Cover photograph © Fotolia.com

# CONTENTS

# PREFACE

## Why don't consultants like appointments?

If I had had this brilliant and compact book by Sarah Fox fifteen years ago, it would have saved my firms hundreds of hours of agony and procrastination. Appointments don't have to be complicated after all.

As a manager of construction services consultancies I was often called in to prepare client appointments, and I soon found out that consultants really don't like appointments!

**We don't like talking about money**

Some consultants feel that we have a vocation, not a career. We aren't doing it for the money, so talking about fees is uncomfortable. That discomfort means we tend to avoid it if we can, even if we know it is important.

**We don't want to put off the client**

When we start talking to a client about their project, we may be just getting to know them, and they us. We think that if we start writing down terms we could scare them off and lose the job or their trust, especially as we think appointments have to be long and complicated. This is why Sarah's book is so useful – it shows you how to write 500-word appointments.

**It's never the right time**

Sooner or later, we realise that we never quite got around to talking to our client about our services and our fees. Before we know it, we are outside the 'right time' territory. We think it is too late, and sorting the details out becomes harder and harder. Sarah's method helps us sort appointments quickly and up front.

### We don't like conflict

When we think about agreeing the terms of our appointment, we worry that we will precipitate a conflict with our client. Although we think contracts are creators of conflict, my experience is that a good appointment can help avoid conflict and is the perfect way to relax clients.

### We don't understand appointments

If your legal training was anything like mine, it mostly consisted of a construction lawyer relishing the experience of recounting to a group of students how he stitched up an architect with a consultant appointment. But you don't need a degree to use a good appointment; it's the appointment that is at fault.

### So why do I recommend Sarah's book?

Let's face it, we don't understand how appointments work, and we're scared of them. I had all these fears, and lost money as a result. If I had had Sarah's book I would have saved myself a lot of heartache, as well as money.

This book explains in simple terms why appointments benefit your client as well as you. It will help you write short effective appointments which deal with all the challenging issues like copyright and cancellations which keep us awake at night, and smooth the process of getting on with the job – which is what we want the most.

Sarah demystified appointment documents for me, and her book will demystify them for you too. I wholeheartedly recommend it to you.

***Su Butcher***

*Just Practising Limited*

# INTRODUCTION

As a consultant providing specialist services to clients, you will need to write your own appointment. An appointment is an agreement between an external supplier and its client, in contrast to acting as an employee.

Existing letters of appointment, conditions of engagement or professional services contracts are designed by professional bodies to suit the needs of their own members. So they tend to be one-sided, risk-averse and complex. They try to cover all types of consultants, from solo practitioners providing one-off services to homeowners, to consulting teams employed by multi-disciplinary practices on million pound developments.

In response, many consultants create their own DIY appointments using a mish-mash of stolen clauses, words to strike fear into clients (so you avoid that issue you had with the snooty Mr Steele four years ago), and random terms 'just because'.

This book is especially for you if you find existing appointments neither meet your needs nor help you do business. It will act as your guide to writing an appointment that is crystal clear, gets your clients to say *Yes* quicker, and protects the interests of both you and your client. In just a few pages, you will learn the critical content your appointment needs and how to use it effectively. You will be guided on how to describe the services you will/will not provide and how much (and when) you will get paid.

## Why Appointments?

Appointments, like all contracts, are tools to *help you do business*. Like any tool in your business tool box, an appointment should provide a solution to your client. Despite most appointments focusing on describing the exchange – the client's money for your services and expertise – each client wants you to solve a specific problem.

Most standard form appointments make little or no mention of this aspect, as solutions are unique to the consultant and cannot be standardised. Your appointment can be a powerful tool to persuade your client that you understand her problem and clearly have the solution she needs. When your client reads it, she is likely to say *Yes* quicker.

## Why 500 Words?

Unlike its longer cousin, a 500-word appointment positively encourages your client to read it and then to agree/negotiate/sign. Your client will understand precisely what she has to do to enable you to help her. Your client will realise that you really understand what she is trying to achieve and will appreciate any risks involved in the project.

In 2012, my twin sister challenged me to write a construction contract in just 500 words: that's a single A4 page. I started from scratch and created a contract that was simple, uncluttered, easy to use, and legally robust. That first contract led onto a series of construction agreements, including an appointment. This book explains how you can write simple and effective appointments too. It will also persuade you to go against the conventional wisdom that length is beneficial and start using simple appointments, by explaining why a 500-word appointment is a good idea.

## Who Should Read This Book?

This book is written for:

- Consultants who write or review their own appointments
- Employers, clients and contractors who want to engage consultants on their own terms
- Advisers who want to understand what an appointment really needs and what can be omitted.

This book focuses on consultants working in the UK construction industry, although the overall messages and direction translate into other industries, countries and specialisms.

Once you have met a prospective client, and she believes you have the expertise to meet her needs, you need to persuade her to use you as her consultant. This requires a combination of a client-specific proposal and a set of more generic terms and conditions. Together they record your agreement. You need to show your client that you understand her needs, are competent and professional, and what she can expect when you work together. You need to make sure your appointment is legally robust and effective – one that both of you can *read, understand and use.*

## The Structure

After explaining what an appointment is, this book is presented in 5 parts:

**Part A: Why you should write simple appointments.** Long appointments (over 30 pages excluding annexes) are the norm in any industry or market, so this Part highlights the benefits of shorter, more readable, more usable appointments. It explains the five legal requirements you need for your appointment to be legally-binding, and why you should use a simple appointment.

**Part B: How you can write client-centred appointments.** This sets out elements your appointment needs that will change for each client. It takes you step-by-step through how to avoid common errors, what happens if you add nothing to your appointment, then why and how you can write it simply.

**Part C: How you can write the challenging content.** Part C explains the three challenging Cs of consultant appointments that cause the most confusion and debate: Copyright, Confidentiality and Cancellation. It takes the same step-by-step approach as Part B.

**Part D: How you can write effective standard terms.** This introduces six effective extras which help you to explain how you and your client are going to work together. It takes the same step-by-step approach as Part B, and covers how to protect your business using effective limits on your liability.

**Part E: Next steps for appointment success.** This summarises how you can plan, create and use your appointment successfully, as well as side-step the showstopper clauses which can bring negotiations to a halt.

The chapters are written in 500-word blocks, to demonstrate that even complex legal issues do not require long-winded explanations. If I can do that with legal issues, you can describe your specialist expertise and services in just 500 words.

## How To Read This Book

The book is short, so it won't take you long to read it. You should read it from start to finish, and mark sections which you know you'll want to return to before you send your next proposal, quote or estimate. You don't need to follow each of the cross-references when you first read the book, as these are just provided for future use. By applying its tips, you will create an appointment that is simple, uncluttered, easy to use, and legally robust.

500 words refers to the *body* of your appointment. How you define the scope of your services and the extent of the project-specific data may take you above the word count.

This book reflects the laws of England/Wales. As a user guide, it is not a comprehensive explanation of all the relevant cases or statutes, nor is it a substitute for legal advice. Depending on your previous experience, you may want to get your lawyer to review your content and check that it is a good fit for your client and her project.

# 1

# WHAT IS AN APPOINTMENT?

An appointment is a contract for services (rather than works, goods or materials). It is often written in the style of a letter and may take the form of anything from a brief electronic instruction to a hard copy booklet.

Irrespective of its form, you will find it easier to write if you plan for it to have three distinct sections:

1. information relating to your client/her project (Part B)
2. clauses which may require adapting or negotiation (Part C), and
3. more generic terms (Part D).

## An Appointment Helps You Do Business

If you are offering consultancy services then, as with other contracts, one purpose of your appointment is to *help you to do business*. It should clearly record what you have agreed with your client. This prevents misunderstandings, and means the appointment acts as a guide to what you (and your client) need to do.

## An Appointment Solves Your Client's Problem

Another purpose of your appointment is to help your client gain specialist expertise from someone with skills, knowledge or experience that she doesn't have (but which she needs). It should clearly outline the expertise you have and how that expertise will help your client.

As non-specialists, clients do not always know what they don't know (sometimes called the 'unknown unknowns').[1] Your client may not know the type of specialist services she needs. Nonetheless, your client *can* articulate the problem she needs help with. Your appointment should explain how your solution (tasks, services, documents, reports, etc.) is a good match for the problem she faces. Your appointment should record how the services you have offered will achieve the results your client needs.

If your appointment is too generic, it can make your client feel like you don't really understand her perspective and are not interested in her project. That's not how you persuade your client to part with her money.

## An Appointment Can Be Amended By Implied Terms

This book considers two types of client involved in a construction[2] project: business clients (companies, partnerships and commercial organisations) and consumers (members of the public).

If your client is a business, then your appointment is probably a 'construction contract'.[3] This means an agreement recording the services you are providing for a building, development or construction project. Terms will be implied into this type of appointment if it does not meet certain minimum requirements. [Chapter 10 on fees and Chapter 20 on adjudication]

If your client is a consumer, then your appointment will not be a construction contract as the project will relate to the construction or extension of your client's own home; but it will be subject to the Consumer Rights Act 2015.[4] Terms will be implied into this type of appointment if you don't make an alternative provision. These terms cover cost, time and quality as well as the binding nature of information on which your client relies. The Act also provides remedies for consumers if the services provided do not meet the criteria set out in the Act. [Chapter 20]

# 2

# TEN FREQUENTLY ASKED QUESTIONS

1 **What can I include in my appointment?** Under English/Welsh law, the parties have freedom to contract which means that you can include anything you like provided you meet the five requirements for a contract. [Chapter 3] A tenant can require a birthday cake in its tenancy agreement[5] a software company can gain your immortal soul[6] or a Wi-Fi provider can take your eldest child.[7]

2 **What is the market norm for payment?** You can agree and then write any fee and payment schedule you like into your appointment. You can ask for your fees in advance or wait 600 days before getting paid. Ideally you would agree a schedule of payments that balances the value and services your client receives with a regular supply of funds for your consultancy, especially if it is with a business client. [Chapter 10]

3 **How can I protect my intellectual property?** Your intellectual property (IP) is contained in the documents, reports, designs, charts, resources and other materials you exchange with your client during the project. The most common protection is through copyright and your appointment should clarify whether you are selling or licensing it, and the limits of that licence. [Chapter 12]

4 **How can I make sure I get paid?** Nothing you write into your appointment will *guarantee* that your client will pay you. It's better to research your client – to check if your client has the financial resources to meet the cost of your fees and any wider project – *before* you sign on the dotted line. However, your appointment can include terms to encourage regular payment, and discourage late payments. [Chapter 17]

5 **How can I write a watertight appointment?** You can't.[8]

6 **How can I protect my business?** Firstly, don't treat your appointment as your *only* safety-net. Your appointment is just one of the means of protecting your business. Secondly, use this book to limit your liability in case of problems. [Chapter 18] Thirdly, choose carefully what work you take on.

7 **Why do disputes happen?** The NBS National Construction Contracts and Law Survey 2015[9] cited the main issues in disputes – relevant to consultant appointments – as *money* and *contract terms*.

8 **What can be done to minimise the risk of disputes?** As well as creating clear payment terms and simplifying your terms (see above), frequent communication with your client is critical to managing her expectations, ensuring she understands how her project is progressing and keeping her updated on any changes.

9 **What's the main risk in *writing* an appointment?** The main risk in writing an appointment is that you do not spell out clearly enough what your client needs to do (if she doesn't understand it, she won't do it), and how your services will solve her problem.

10 **What's the main risk in *using* an appointment?** The main risk is that you shove it in a drawer and never re-read it. As a consultant you may forget what you have agreed to provide, and your client may not realise how her actions can adversely affect other aspects of the project.

# PART A

# WHY YOU SHOULD WRITE SIMPLE APPOINTMENTS

This Part explains why your appointment needs to be a legally-binding contract.

Whether you are writing an appointment for a consumer or a commercial client, this Part explains three key reasons why that appointment should be simple:

1 **To manage expectations.** The whole purpose of recording your agreement is to manage the expectations of your client. Chapter 4 explains how your simple appointment will help you avoid misunderstandings and distrust, as the client can understand precisely how you solve her problems.

2 **To limit the scope of your agreement.** The most effective way to limit and exclude your liability – while at the same time providing a clear record of what you and your client have agreed – is to accurately record what you are and are not doing. Chapter 5 describes how.

3 **To avoid disputes.** English/Welsh law requires consumer contracts to be written in plain and intelligible language and be legible (this is what the Consumer Rights Act 2015 calls 'transparent'). This is good practice for business contracts too. Plain language means that your client can find what she needs, understand what she finds and use what she finds to meet her needs.[10] If you want to avoid disputes, then Chapter 6 shows that you need to write an appointment that you and your client can read, understand and use.

There is little point going to the effort of creating an appointment if some of its terms could be struck out by the court. A simple appointment will minimise the risk that any of the terms are unfair or unreasonable. [Chapter 18]

By the end of this Part, you should be convinced that you need to spend time writing a simple appointment (using Parts B, C and D).

# 3

# WHAT IS A CONTRACT?

A contract is a legally-binding agreement; a promise that can be relied on and enforced. It doesn't need any specific form, words or style. It doesn't even need to be written down ... although as Samuel Goldwyn is reputed to have said:

> *A verbal contract isn't worth the paper it's written on.*

The vast majority of appointments *are* contracts. To be legally-binding, your appointment has to satisfy these five legal requirements:

1. A clear **Offer** to pay for specific services
2. **Acceptance** of that offer, either by signed returned document or by doing something
3. **Consideration** means exchanging your services for something of value
4. An **Intention** to create a legally-binding contract *now*
5. **Certain** and essential terms.

Once an offer has been accepted, then you have created an *agreement*. (Although the terms agreement and contract are used interchangeably, not all agreements are contracts.) All the above five legal requirements are *essential* for your appointment to be a contract.

In practice, these requirements are surprisingly easy to meet. Before you work for a new client, she will often ask you to send her a proposal, quote or estimate:

- Your proposal is an *offer* to carry out specific services for that client.
- Your proposal can be *accepted* by email, telephone call, by your client signing your appointment or paying your first invoice.
- Your proposal asks for *something of value* (often money) in return for those services. What lawyers call *consideration* – the price or a promise to do something – is anything of value and can be as inconsequential as a peppercorn or a used sweet wrapper.

The first three legal requirements are easily ticked off. When it comes to intention, the rules differ depending on whether your transaction is business-to-business (B2B) or business-to-consumer (B2C).

- If your proposal is B2B then *the intention to create a contract* is presumed to exist.
- If your proposal is B2C, then English/Welsh law adds a 14-day Cooling-off Period[11] for contracts made at your client's home or by email. This ensures your client wants to enter into this contract, and is not being pressured or bullied into it.

The last requirement – *certainty* – is the most difficult aspect for appointment writers and it is where you should focus your attention (Part B).

**Why Do You Need Certain Terms?** Your appointment should set out what the parties have agreed with certainty.

Your appointment needs to provide certainty for the *parties*. Your client wants to know how much she will have to pay for your services, and you want to know which services are included in your fee (and which are extras). Certainty ensures both parties know precisely what they have to do.

Your appointment should also provide certainty for *outsiders*, so that an independent person (e.g. a judge) can immediately understand everything that both parties have agreed to do. If your appointment only makes sense because of information you personally have inside your head, then a court may not be able to interpret it or enforce it.

# 4

# SIMPLE APPOINTMENTS MANAGE EXPECTATIONS

The main purposes of an appointment are (1) to help you do business, and (2) to help your client gain specialist expertise. Even if you have been in business for many years, your client may never have done this sort of project before. Just because you have always done it your way, doesn't mean your client wants to do it that way. An appointment needs to clarify the roles and responsibilities of your client and you, as her consultant.

It is a trite saying that *To assume makes an ass out of u and me.* Nonetheless, many disputes arise precisely because the parties made assumptions about one or more aspects of the project including:

- What your client really wants to achieve (but you never asked)
- What you think your client doesn't want but she actually does (and believes you are providing as part of your services for the agreed fees)
- The facilities, instructions, approval and directions your client should be responsible for (as an expert it is not enough to hope your client realises what is required)
- Who is responsible for procuring other services, goods, materials or consents needed to complete the project (that you cannot provide)

- How often and through what means you will communicate with your client
- What happens when your client is feeling unhappy with your services, progress or the result. A clear process for discussing issues can nip potential disputes in the bud.

For a consumer contract, English/Welsh law requires you to provide various items of information before your client signs on the dotted line and this is the bare minimum: main characteristics of your services, your contact details[12], the price she will have to pay (including taxes), when you will perform the services, your complaints handling policy, and how long your appointment will last.

### All That Is Gold Does Not Glitter

A millionaire businessman dreamed of the construction of an Arts and Craft style house to be called Maison d'Or (House of Gold) in St Aubin, Jersey. It took 3 years to build at a cost of £4m and the client was so unhappy, he demolished it. The court recorded the absence of 'certain documents and procedures which are generally regarded as critical to a satisfactory outcome' like contracts and a specification.

*One of the features of this case is the absence of any written record of what Mr McGlinn wanted at the outset and, in particular, what standard of finish he required at Maison d'Or … a point he repeatedly made was that it had not been designed or built in accordance with the exceptionally high standards that he had asked for. This, inevitably, led to numerous disputes as to what precisely it was that he had required, given the absence of any written record or clear design brief.*

The court agreed that the deficiencies in the contracting process offered an easy explanation of why things went wrong and why the project did not meet the client's expectations.[13]

# 5

# SIMPLE APPOINTMENTS LIMIT YOUR AGREEMENT

Like any contract, your appointment should accurately, briefly and concisely describe what you and your client have agreed. A precise record is one of the best ways of limiting your liability as it clearly sets out the tasks that each of you is, and is not, responsible for.

Most appointments clearly set out specific services and the fees payable. Your appointment should also describe any documents being provided. It should accurately record which person is responsible for which documents, and the rights granted over those documents. Even for a one-off task such as carrying out a survey, gaining planning permission or designing a porch, your appointment needs to guide the parties on what each needs to do.

You must check that your appointment:

- **Sets out specific services:** You should avoid meaningless and vague phrases like 'supervision' or a sweep-up statement like 'all services necessary to administer the building contract'. Accuracy is essential to ensure that variations to those services can be properly charged for.

> **TIP:** Check that you and your client can tell when the services are complete. [Chapter 9]

- **Agrees how the services can be changed:** Under English/Welsh law, an appointment – and the services under that appointment – cannot be varied except by creating a new contract. As this is impractical, it is simpler to include a procedure allowing changes to the services and how the revised fees will be set. Your client would prefer no surprises so any extra fees should be agreed before you implement the changes. If your process is too complex or impractical, it can be circumvented.[14]

> **TIP:** Check that your process means your client will know in advance that she will pay for any changes to the services. [Chapter 19]

- **Defines responsibility for areas outside your expertise:** Your appointment should precisely describe the limits of your responsibility, by clarifying what you are not responsible for. Otherwise your client may (mistakenly) assume you are doing everything she needs. This clarity helps to manage your client's expectations, and sometimes to agree fees for those extras.

> **TIP:** Check your appointment limits the scope of your services. [Chapter 9]

- **Describes the rights you have over documents being exchanged:** Most people find the ownership of the intellectual property in a physical item hard to understand, especially as it is not the same as possession of that item. Your appointment should explain the limits of your client's right to use your copyright material; e.g. for other similar projects or for a specific period.

> **TIP:** Check your appointment limits your client's use of your copyright material. [Chapter 12]

- **Contains an escape clause:** If you discover that your client cannot and will not pay for the services you have provided, or if your client discovers that you are incompetent, or it becomes apparent that your client's project is doomed, it is better to end your contractual relationship swiftly. Your appointment is not intended to be an agreement to work together indefinitely!

**TIP:** Check that your appointment includes a cancellation period [Chapter 14] as well as a mutual right to terminate. [Chapter 20]

# 6

# SIMPLE APPOINTMENTS AVOID DISPUTES

If you create an appointment that is easy to use then you will minimise disputes over money and if you create an appointment that is easy to read and easy to understand then you can avoid disputes relating to contract terms.

**Easy to Read:** Your appointment will be easy to read if it has clear headings, short sentences and simple words. It is a myth that contracts need to be complex.

A 500-word appointment helps you avoid disputes because:

- *Your client will read it*: the short length of your appointment will encourage your client to read it from start to finish.
- *Your client can negotiate it*: an easy-to-read appointment acts as a checklist for negotiation.
- *Your client can be sure it records what you have agreed*: simple words mean your client can immediately check whether the document is an accurate reflection of your agreement.

If your client does not read your appointment, then she definitely won't understand it.

**Easy to Understand:** Your appointment will be easy to understand if it avoids the jargon, legalese and technical terms prevalent in most contracts. It is a myth that only lawyers should be able to understand the scope and impact of your appointment.

A 500-word appointment helps you avoid disputes because:

- *Your client will have the confidence to raise queries*: with clear and crisp content, your client knows what each word and each paragraph means, and will not be afraid to check if something does not make sense.
- *Your client will take responsibility*: when your appointment is easy to understand and non-threatening, then you can resolve issues quickly, without the need to get lawyers involved.

If your client does not understand your appointment, then she definitely won't know what she is meant to do and when.

**Easy to Use:** Your appointment will be easy to use if it is designed with the parties in mind. It is a myth that contracts should cover everything the parties can possibly think of, resulting in tedious length. Once your appointment contains just four items – parties, services, aims and fees – it is long enough.

A 500-word appointment helps you avoid disputes because:

- *Your appointment builds trust*: when both parties can use your appointment, they are more likely to search for ways to make it work, which naturally helps you to be more collaborative.
- *Your client will want to comply*: a clear appointment leaves no scope for debate about what your client is meant to do/pay and when.

These changes can minimise the disputes arising from the content of your appointment, as well as build better relationships with your clients. Your appointment should record what is required to enable you to carry out the services and meet your client's *needs*, and do so accurately, briefly and clearly.

# PART B

# HOW YOU CAN WRITE CLIENT-CENTRED APPOINTMENTS

The bare minimum needed for an appointment to create certainty, and be legally-binding, is as simple as who, what, why and how much?

If your appointment does not state the parties and the services, then it does not have enough certainty to be a contract. If your appointment does not state how much your client is paying or why she is bothering (i.e. the problem you are going to solve), then you may have a contract but it won't provide clarity for your client.

Part B will show that an indispensable element of creating a client-centred appointment is to explain *how your services solve your client's needs*. These are the four client-centred contents you need (which vary with each client):

- **WHO? THE PARTIES:** your appointment should explain the person, people or business that is paying for the services (your client) and who is carrying them out (you, as the consultant).
- **WHAT? THE SERVICES:** your appointment should specify precisely the services that will meet your client's needs.
- **WHY? THE AIMS:** your appointment should clarify how your services will achieve your client's objectives or aims.
- **HOW MUCH? THE FEES:** your appointment should describe how much your client will pay for your services and when.

This Part will help you understand what to write in your appointment and why you should keep it simple. Each chapter looks at some of the risks of not writing each element simply and what happens if your appointment includes nothing on that topic.

# 7

# BEFORE YOU START WRITING YOUR APPOINTMENT

There are a number of stages to writing any document, and these apply to appointments from 2 pages (like a 500-word appointment) to 200 pages long.

- **Readers:** Your appointment will be read by the parties, legal and business advisers, and, if you're unlucky, a judge. You should write it to be read by all those people.
- **Users:** You and your client actually have to use your appointment, so make it user-friendly.
- **Your Purpose:** There are a number of different purposes for your appointment (see below) and you need to decide before you start which you are going to focus on.
- **Content:** This book sets out what content your appointment needs. Part B sets out the four client-centred contents, Part C the three challenging Cs, and Part D the six effective extras. You should only start writing when you know what you need.
- **Order:** Despite myths to the contrary, there is no fixed structure or order for the contents of your appointment (or any contract). To make sure it gets read first, you should explain how your services meet your client's needs at the start of your appointment, and then

add the rest of the client-centred contents. You can group the client and consultant obligations into separate sections to make them easy to find. Clauses that apply to both parties, such as copyright and confidentiality, and those that explain how changes, disputes and termination are dealt with would follow.

- **Write:** How you write your appointment is a matter of preference – typed, dictated or hand-written all have the same end result. You can even create it in graphic form.[15] The key is to start from a blank piece of paper and use this book to write down just what you think your appointment really needs, and then stop. *Do not recycle a previously used document!*
- **Edit:** This is how you check that it contains the contents you think are essential, as well as ensuring your appointment is accurate, brief and clear.

## What Is Your Purpose?

Many appointment writers never stop and think *why* they are writing and using them. A specific purpose will focus your writing making it clearer and crisper.

Do you want your appointment to:

- *protect only your interests* ('cover your back')? A one-sided document is likely to be unfair, cause friction or confuse your client. It is better to create an appointment which balances and protects both your interests.
- *be watertight or bombproof*? Sadly, there is no such thing.
- *act as a form of insurance* in the event of a complaint or dispute? If so, you are missing the opportunity to guide your client on how to behave while you are working together. It should not merely be a document which explains how to 'clean up' afterwards.

The true purpose of an appointment is to *clarify* the scope of the services to be carried out and the fees to be paid, your/your client's aims, and how risk is to be managed.

# 8

# THE PARTIES INVOLVED

Recording the identity of the parties accurately on your appointment is the easiest part – just like addressing a letter or email to the right recipient. It doesn't matter who they are. In English/Welsh law you are free to contract with just about *anyone.*[16]

Once you name 'the Consultant' on your appointment that business will be legally obliged to carry out the services. The court is rarely persuaded that errors in the parties' names allow them to escape liability under your appointment. The identity of 'the Client' is a matter of practicality. As tempting as it is to stick to electronic means of sending documents, if your only contact details are a mobile number and email address, your client may prove hard to contact and harder to sue.

## Avoiding Common Errors

To ensure your appointment names the parties correctly, you should:

- Use clear, sufficient and correct business details (see over), especially if you are part of a large group of similarly-named companies or have an unusual partnership structure.
- Create an electronic, digital or hard copy appointment for signing.

- Ensure each person who signs the appointment is correctly authorised to sign. In practice if the wrong person signs for the consultant and your client entered into the appointment in good faith, the courts will allow your client to enforce it.
- Make sure joint clients sign independently of the other, where relevant.
- Ensure you send a signed copy of your appointment to your client.

Generally, errors relating to the identity of the parties can be solved by the courts as most appointments follow an enquiry, proposal, discussion and correspondence trail during which the parties' names are disclosed.

## Does It Really Matter?

### Passing On Your Responsibilities

A developer client appointed a consultant structural engineer to design the foundations and floor slab for a new £2m supermarket in Sandwich, Kent. Site surveys noted that the ground required specific foundations to meet the project's needs. The consultant worked with and approved the designs of a specialist subcontractor (appointed by the contractor). Within months of completion, the floor and tiling in the supermarket started to crack and the client claimed £3m to rebuild the store. The consultant argued that by using a specialist subcontractor it was not liable.

The court said:

*(1) That construction professionals [the consultants] do not by the mere act of obtaining advice or a design from another party thereby divest themselves of their duties in respect of that advice or design …*

*(2) That construction professionals can discharge their duty to take reasonable care by relying on the advice or design of a specialist provided that they act reasonably in doing so …*

**Was it reasonable?**

Although the court held the consultant was not liable (as the foundations it designed could have met the project's needs as set out in the specification), it decided that it had acted reasonably in working with a recognised expert.[17]

**Do You Need To Include The Parties?** Yes. If your appointment does not correctly identify the parties responsible for carrying out its obligations, then it lacks certainty and is not a contract. Getting the parties right is *critical.*

**Why Should You Keep It Simple?** There are five reasons you should keep it simple. Firstly, it is incredibly quick to clarify the correct details for the parties; secondly, getting it right means you know precisely which business, individual or people you are contracting with; thirdly, the consequences of getting it wrong are significant; and fourthly, legislation requires you to give correct information to consumer clients.[18]

The final reason to be clear about the parties to the appointment is technical (in the legal sense). In English/Welsh law, a principle called 'privity of contract' means only those parties listed on the appointment can bring claims against each other.[19] You cannot sue Ms Smith who gave you instructions, nor the bank loaning money for the project, if they are not named as your client on your appointment. Similarly, your client cannot sue your employees or sub-consultants as her rights are only against you. Knowing with whom you are entering into an appointment is relatively simple, legally critical and practically essential.

**How You Can Write It Simply:** Your appointment should correctly record three things:

1. the identity of the parties
2. the geographical addresses (plus telephone and email address) for notices

**3** one of:

- the company name, registered number and registered office[20] *for corporations (including limited liability partnerships or LLPs)*
- the partnership name, the name of all current partners and the principal office *for partnerships*
- the trading name, the owner and the place of business *for a sole trader*
- their full names and addresses *for individuals.*

If your appointment is designed as a letter, then the 'consultant information' is generally found on your letterhead or in your email signature. You should add the client information in the heading to the appointment, and addresses for notices for both parties can be added into the appointment as a separate paragraph.

As well as naming the parties, your appointment should be signed on behalf of each party by a properly authorised person. In England/Wales that means:

- a director or company secretary *for corporations (including LLPs)*
- all or a specific number of partners (as set out in their partnership agreement) *for partnerships*
- the owner or each person *for a sole trader/individuals.*

Partners, directors and company representatives sign as agents for that business and your appointment is treated as made by the company or partnership. This method of signing creates a Simple Contract [Glossary] and the parties can bring claims for its breach for 6 years from the last day when services were provided.

Signing your appointment is best practice as it shows the parties have agreed to all the terms in that document. In practice, your appointment can actually be accepted by email, telephone or when you start to provide the services.

# 9

# THE SERVICES YOU ARE PROVIDING

Your appointment is the tool that will enable your client to get specialist expertise to meet a particular need. Your client will want to know what services you are providing, that you are competent to provide them, and that those services will help her to achieve a specific objective. [Chapter 11]

Are you:

- Designing a new house extension?
- Advising about obligations under health and safety legislation?
- Supervising the contractor carrying out the project?
- Surveying a newly constructed property to check it meets Building Regulations?
- Collaborating during a design workshop to offer possible solutions?
- None of the above?

## Avoiding Common Errors

To ensure your appointment identifies your services precisely you should describe the services so you, your client and an outsider can tell when everything that you promised to do has been completed.

This can be done by listing:

- Any stages of the project you will provide regular services for; e.g. supervision, attendance or certification
- All the documents or materials that you will be providing: layouts, reports, analysis, advice, drawings, plans, guidance, cost schedules, and less tangible items such as copyright, moral rights, electronic documents, etc.
- The distinct tasks and jobs that you need to perform (such as providing the client with information for planning)
- The project outputs for different elements of your services; e.g. approval of third parties, appointment of a contractor, or the completion of defects.

Your description of the services should ensure that the client knows what you are doing and when. Some appointments take a vague or broad-brush approach which means your client has no idea what you are actually doing.

A good appointment will provide a description of the services which is both succinct and sophisticated. Your services should be clearly defined in terms that both parties can understand. If your client has never used a consultant before then using jargon or technical terms will dissuade her from reading your services and can slow down the process of agreeing the terms.

## Does It Really Matter?

### It's Not Enough To Be Vague

A large multi-disciplinary consulting firm was appointed by the Trustees of a college to act as their project managers on a series of projects to create new accommodation at the school. Sadly, the client's requirements for the projects to be completed in time for a new school term were not met and the client sued the consultant for failing in its duties.

## Be Precise

The court said the project manager's precise role should have been properly defined by the terms of its appointment. A *central part of the role of the project manager [was] as co-ordinator and guardian of the client's interests*. The court acknowledged the difficulty in constructing *'a detailed prescriptive account of precisely what steps should have been taken and when they should have been taken'* (which the appointment lacked), and focused on whether the project manager's performance of its appointment met the required standard of reasonable care and skill.[21]

**Do You Need To Include The Services?** Yes. If your appointment does not identify the services, your appointment is too uncertain to be a contract. Hastily prepared appointments asking consultants to *carry out the usual services for the usual fees* are ineffective for all practical *and* legal purposes. This is a real example I was once sent by a client and, although succinct, it didn't tell me what the consultant actually did!

That's not quite the end of the story though. Once you start to provide services following a client request, from which your client benefits, then your client *will* to have to pay for those services. A principle known as 'unjust enrichment' prevents your client taking the benefit of those services for free. You can claim payment of 'a reasonable sum'.[22]

**Why Should You Keep It Simple?** Your appointment should be an agreement between two parties for your client to pay you to provide specific services at a defined price. Without a clear scope of services, how can you possibly:

- decide a fair price to be paid?
- determine what are or are not extra services, which entitle you to an extra fee?
- agree how those services will meet your client's needs?
- know when you have finished (often linked to the final payment)?

**How You Can Write It Simply:** For most clients, you are carrying out one of a range of services you have provided before. You are the best person to describe precisely what you will do for this client.

After you have been in business for a while, you can create a checklist of your usual services and adapt that checklist. Your appointment can describe your services and any documents you will provide accurately, briefly and clearly:

The Consultant will provide the Services <insert>.

Your appointment will be accurate if the description of the services makes sense to the parties and other people. It needs to have enough detail and information to allow an outsider to decide whether you have done what you were asked to do. The list of services should state documents, resources or other items your client is expecting.

It will be more accurate (and limit your scope) if it also says clearly what you are *not* going to do. This is a simple means of excluding your responsibility for tasks outside your expertise, which others should undertake, or to clarify possible areas of overlap. Your appointment can say *The Consultant will neither provide nor be responsible for <insert tasks, services or elements of the project>.*

Your appointment will be brief and clear if it contains all the necessary information without ambiguities or inconsistencies. While it may be tempting to add broad descriptions of your services, this may result in the client expecting you to provide more services than you intended (and priced for). For larger projects, your list of services is never going to be 100% comprehensive, but writing it simply can ensure your client reads your outline and understands your role.

# 10

# THE FEES YOUR CLIENT WILL PAY

The problem with talking money is that everyone *thinks* they are hard done to.

The problem with *not* talking money is that everyone *will definitely* be hard done to!

Many disputes revolve around whether a client has paid what she promised and a consultant has provided the services it promised. Knowing how much is to be paid and when is crucial to both parties. Of the top 11 main issues in dispute mentioned in the NBS National Construction Contracts and Law Survey 2015[23], seven relate to money:

1. Valuation of a final account
2. Valuation of variations (extras)
3. Loss and expense (claims for money for prolonged projects)
4. Failure to comply with payment provisions
5. Withholding monies
6. Valuation of interim payments
7. Non-payment of fees.

Some of these are directly applicable to appointments; e.g. not complying with the payment procedure, withholding fees and non-payment of fees. A simple procedure can help make it easier for your client to pay the right amounts on time.

## Avoiding Common Errors

Your appointment should:

- state the basis on which your fees will be paid, and this may be a combination of a fixed price for specific services, a percentage of the project cost or an hourly rate (paid on a time-spent basis)
- state how much your client will pay including tax[24], if known in advance
- state how your fees will be split into instalments - either based on percentages of the services carried out, specific dates, or completion of stages of the services
- include fees/an hourly rate for additional services to enable extras to be priced before you carry them out.

If your appointment lacks clarity on *services, fees and commencement*, you are effectively asking the client to sign up to open-ended liability to pay for an open-ended set of tasks to be started when you choose.

If your client is a business, your appointment should also meet the minimum requirements for payment set out in the Construction Acts 1996 and 2009.

## Does It Really Matter?

### As Long As A Piece Of String

For the refurbishment of their Grade II Listed late-Georgian country house, Bengeo Hall, Mr Cunningham and Ms Good appointed a firm of architects. The architect quoted fees based on a projected construction cost of £300,000. The court said *the evidence was that everybody, including Mr Cunningham, knew and accepted that that figure was purely notional, included in the letter for the sole purpose of fees calculation.*[25]

The fees in the appointment were 11.75% of the now £525,000 construction sum, and 10% of any increases on that construction sum 'for the sake of simplicity'. This was up to a *total maximum fee payable for works to main house, boundary fence and garden wall [of] £70,000 plus VAT and expenses.*

The court noted that the architect might have been out of pocket had the project continued (as it was over budget and running late) but *that was a risk that they ran when they switched to a fixed monthly amount and a maximum entitlement.*

**Do You Need To Include Fees?** There are two aspects to consider: *what* you want your client to pay for the services and *how* you want them to pay.

If your appointment does not contain your fees, or a means of determining fees, it *may* be too uncertain for a contract. But once you get started, even if you have not yet agreed your fees, legislation implies a term that your client will pay a reasonable charge or reasonable price for your services.[26]

For consumer clients, you are free to decide how and when you want your client to pay your fees. For business clients, legislation entitles you to be paid by instalments, stage payments or periodic payments[27] and implies relevant terms if you fail to include them.

**Why Should You Keep It Simple?** If you don't agree and state your fees in your appointment, then your client has no idea what her payment obligation is and you have no idea whether you are going to get properly compensated. A consumer client can challenge the level of your fees if they are not prominent and transparent. A business client may refuse to pay if your fees are not clear.

Once you have decided what your client is going to pay, your appointment needs a simple payment procedure. The more complex it is, the less likely your client will follow it. If your business client doesn't pay on time, you have an implied right to suspend your services, and charge interest on late payments. Relying on these remedies can destroy your relationship with your client irrevocably. It is far better to have simple procedures that anyone can follow.

**How You Can Write It Simply:** For consumer clients, the simplest way to write *what* and *how* your client has to pay, is to set out a schedule of payments with fixed prices for different elements:

> The Client will pay the Fees £<insert> quickly and fairly against correct Consultant invoices as set out in the Payment Schedule.[28]

For business clients, your appointment needs more detail including payment notices and pay-less notices [Glossary], as well as your right to suspend the services for non-payment:

> The Consultant will send invoices following the Payment Schedule stating the sum it considers payable and its calculation. At least <5> days before the final date, the Client will send a written pay-less notice if she intends to pay less than the invoiced amount showing how much she will pay and her calculation. If the Client neither sends a pay-less notice nor pays in full, the Consultant may suspend carrying out any of the Services until paid in full, without being liable for delays to the Project as a result of that suspension.

## Payment Schedule

The first invoice for £<amount> will be sent by <date>. Future invoices will be sent as below: <insert table with dates and amounts>. Due dates are <insert> days after invoice receipt and final dates are <insert> days after receipt.

# 11

# THE EXPECTATIONS YOU NEED TO MEET

There are three categories of expectations that your appointment needs to take account of:

**Core Expectations:** Cost, time and quality are referred in project management circles as the iron triangle and are often measured to ascertain the success of a construction project. They apply whatever the size, style or shape of your client's project. Your appointment has to strike a balance between getting the services started and finished quickly, at a price that your client can afford yet reflects the value you will provide, and to the quality standards your client desires and you can meet. These are covered in Chapters 10, 15 and 16 respectively.

**Client Specific:** While every project contains certain run-of-the-mill aspects, each client has her own needs and aims (her *why*). Some of these may also be guided by your marketing materials and pre-contract information. Under the Consumer Rights Act 2015, a consumer client is entitled to rely on the pre-contract information that you provide to her as being a binding term of your appointment.

**Trust:** Although each party has its own individual *why*, everyone involved in a project has to work together. You will need to share information and documents, be honest with each other as to the resources you have or your client needs, provide accurate data and instructions on time, and not prevent others from getting on with their tasks. Trust is essential to construction, as it is an inherently collaborative process, with everyone working to a common goal.

## Avoiding Common Errors

Your appointment should not:

- Ignore the problem that your client seeks a solution to. It is far too easy to rush headlong into providing what she asked for without checking that it is what she needs. This is where asking great questions is critical. [Chapter 21]
- Overlook the importance of trust. Your appointment should not treat your client as an adversary, or attempt to ensure you retain the legal and moral high ground. You need to set out how you and your client will work together.

### Does It Really Matter?

#### Avoid Disasters

Mr and Mrs West asked an architect practice to supervise extensive works to their new home, which turned into a disaster. Damp (spotted before the house purchase) was never properly verified and the clients' aim of a sleek renovation was not achieved. The architect had a jaundiced view of his clients, referring to Mr West as 'fancy pants' and accusing him of 'huffing' about design issues. This attitude did not help the consultant meet the client's needs or trust each other.

The court said that *in the context of a domestic building contract, the emotional commitment of the employer is invariably high and so the demands on the contractor and architect are correspondingly increased: the maintenance of good relations between employer, architect and builder is therefore crucial.*[29]

## CLIENT SPECIFIC AIMS

**Do You Need Aims?** If you don't state what your client wants to achieve then your appointment will be certain enough to be a contract, but you will never know if the project and your role in it was a success.

**Why Should You Keep It Simple?** Your client doesn't really care about the letters after your name, what previous clients say about you, or how big your office is. She wants to know that you can solve her problem. If your appointment makes no reference to her aims, how can she check that you have properly understood her needs? A simple statement of her challenge or the aims of her project will manage her expectations and set the foundations for success.

**How You Can Write It Simply:** As each client is different, you need to reflect back on what your client explained when you asked her why she was doing this project and the problems she needs you to solve. You can simply record these as: *Your expectations are <insert>. If our understanding of your project is wrong or incomplete, please let us know immediately.*

## TRUST

**Do You Need To Trust Your Client?** In law, *no*. In practice, *yes*.

Many appointments seem to be designed for the small percentage of clients who are difficult to deal with, pay late, never provide instructions, complain bitterly over the slightest slip, and make the life of a consultant unpleasant. This approach *assumes* your client will act badly. Surely it is better to have good expectations of all your clients, while being realistic enough to know that sometimes you will be disappointed.

If you are working on a construction project, there is an implied obligation on the parties to co-operate with each other. You cannot help your client if she does not provide you access to survey the site, information about her needs, instructions and approvals. Your client cannot achieve her aims and expectations if you don't keep communicating with each other.

**Why Should You Keep It Simple?** Although you and your client understand in principle that trust is essential, sometimes you and your client (and even the project team) can forget that you are all in this *together*. Collaboration, trust, and integrity do not come naturally to everyone.

Your appointment can simply set out the behaviours you expect from your client and your client expects from you, to build your credibility and demonstrate your competence.

**How You Can Write It Simply:** Even clients and contractors with considerable experience can be surprised when they find out they are *obliged* to work together to complete a project. Your appointment can spell out your understanding of your client's role and the conduct you expect from her. You can set your project on the right course by simply stating:

> This appointment records the parties agreeing to work together on the Project. The key aim of the Project is <pick one of cost, time or quality; or insert another>.

# PART C

# HOW YOU CAN WRITE THE CHALLENGING CONTENT

Once your appointment meets the five legal requirements (Part A) and contains the four client-centred contents (Part B), it will be a legally-binding agreement. As a result it creates obligations on both you and your client. If either party does not meet those obligations, the other can bring a claim for breach of the appointment.

Although the main elements that you need to tailor to each client are set out in Part B, there are three elements that vary depending on your relationship with your client. These are:

- **Copyright:** As a consultant you need to control the use of your intellectual property, most commonly through copyright. It is usual to license your client to use the copyright in the documents or designs you produce, and this licence can then be restricted to specific acts or projects. You can also assign copyright to a client absolutely. [Chapter 12]
- **Confidentiality:** Increasingly you may be asked, particularly by larger business clients, to sign 'non-disclosure agreements' or complex confidentiality provisions. Consumers, on the other hand, tend to rely on trust. You will need to decide how to reflect this disparity in your appointment. [Chapter 13]
- **Cancellation:** Your client may want the option to cancel any future services under your appointment without any specific trigger. As your appointment gives you the right to carry out all the services, this should be restricted to specific stages of the services; e.g. after your planning application, before your survey or works start. And it should always entitle you to recover a fair payment to reflect the services already provided. If your client is a consumer, then your appointment must also include a short Cooling-off Period. [Chapter 14]

Freedom to contract means the choice of options for each of these challenging areas is yours. Before you start negotiating the details of your appointment, you should decide what terms you would like to agree to as part of a clear contract strategy. Too often, discussions about terms and key issues are left until you are emotionally (if not financially) committed to the project, leaving you little room to manoeuvre and your preferred balance of terms tilted to one side or the other.

# 12

# PROTECTING YOUR COPYRIGHT

Intellectual property is the name for the intangible property in things such as brands, logos, products you invent, documents that you write and designs you create. It has to be unique and it has to be physically recorded (ideas cannot be protected). Every medium (documents, audio, video, photographs, etc.) contains the expression of your ideas, and that form of expression can attract copyright.

As the UK government says: *Copyright protects your work and stops others from using it without your permission.*[30]

Design right and copyright exist automatically[31] and do not need to be registered, unlike trademarks, registered designs and patents. Controlling the use of your copyright is critical to your business. You can (but don't need to) mark your work with the copyright symbol, your name and the year of creation – known as the 'copyright legend' like this one: © Sarah Fox 2017.

Copyright covers a wide range of documents and media including:

- Illustrations and photographs
- Software, databases and digital project models
- Sketches, design and plans

- Video and audio recordings
- Reports, surveys and proposals.

Your intellectual property is one of the core elements of your business and you should not give it away lightly. Copyright prevents your client (and those to whom she passes your work) from copying, distributing, selling, lending, adapting it, or adding it to web-pages. Whenever a document attracts copyright it also attracts certain moral rights which include the rights to be identified as the author and to object to changes or derogatory treatment.

## Avoiding Common Errors

The most common error is not to agree with your client how she can use the documents you create in the course of your appointment. You have to decide between selling the copyright in your documents to your client (when you lose control), or licensing her to copy those documents (when you keep control and she gets the rights she needs).

## Does It Really Matter?

### Waiting 40 Years For Clarity

In 2009 the UK Supreme Court decided that Matthew Fisher, a musician, was entitled to a share of musical copyright relating to *A Whiter Shade of Pale* by Procul Harum (a record released over 40 years previously, in 1967). It was *one of the most successful popular songs of the late 1960s*, and it is *no exaggeration to say that with the passage of time the song has achieved something approaching cult status.*[32]

Mr Fisher had created the organ solo (or riff) which differed from the music composed by Mr Gary Brooker. The court had to decide whether what he had done was unique and whether he had waived his rights under a recording contract (signed when he was still a minor). His copyright was recognised many years after the parties should have resolved it in a contract.

> **Permission to Copy**
>
> In a different case, the court held that an appointment which results in copyright material being produced *implies a permission, or consent, or licence … to use the material in the manner and for the purpose in which and for which it was contemplated between the parties that it would be used.*[33]

**Do You Need To Include Copyright?** No. Your appointment will be legally-binding. Legislation says that you retain copyright even if you are commissioned to provide bespoke documents, unless you agree otherwise. A licence will be implied (under case law) entitling your client to use the copyright work, and the licence is limited to 'the extent necessary to achieve the intentions of the parties at the time the work was commissioned'[34]. Another reason, if you needed one, to set out your expectations in the appointment. [Chapter 11]

An implied licence only applies once your client has paid your fees for the related services.

**Why Should You Keep It Simple?** As the music case demonstrates, not only is intellectual property highly valuable, its ownership is not always obvious. Confusion arises between ownership of the physical document such as a plan, and ownership of the copyright in that document.

For example, once your client has paid for your plans, she owns those plans but not necessarily the copyright in them. You should be clear how she can use them without being in breach of your licence.

A very wide licence or sale of your intellectual property could damage your business, as it may include intellectual property in documents which you created before this appointment, but which contributed to the copyright documents. Such a licence is wide enough to cover your expertise to date!

**How You Can Write It Simply:** If you have created documents specifically for your client's project, then your copyright licence should limit use to this project and exclude liability for extended uses (the documents may not be suitable for other projects):

> Copyright in all documents, designs and information prepared by the Consultant for the Project belongs to the Consultant. The Consultant licenses the Client non-exclusively without royalties to use, copy and share those documents for all Project purposes except any extension of the Project.[35] The Consultant's liability is limited to the purposes for which those documents were originally prepared.

Most consumer clients have little interest in or awareness of copyright issues. Business clients are very different and are often seeking to protect their long-term interests. You need to be more careful when dealing with businesses. If your copyright documents are based on proprietary processes, the licence should not be limited to one client (an exclusive licence). If your copyright documents could become out-of-date then you should restrict the time period of the licence. If your client is a global business, you may want to restrict the licence to a specific geographical area. The middle sentence above would be changed to state:

> The Consultant licenses the Client non-exclusively without royalties to use, copy and share those documents for all Project purposes for <insert> years from creation and only within <geographical area>.

If you still have significant unresolved intellectual property concerns, you should speak to an expert as this is a complex area of law with serious ramifications for the unwary.

# 13

# PROTECTING CONFIDENTIAL INFORMATION

*It is trite law that equity imposes a duty of confidence when information which has the necessary quality of confidence is communicated in circumstances giving rise to an obligation of confidence.*[36]

The circularity of this statement highlights some of the difficulties with protecting confidential information in the modern business era. Thankfully the quote continues more clearly saying: *The duty prevents unauthorised use of the information to the detriment of the person communicating it.*

You may be asked to sign a confidentiality agreement (also known as a non-disclosure agreement) before a business client will share information with you. This is rare in the construction industry. If you need a 'keep it secret' or non-disclosure agreement, there is a wide variety available from the gov.uk website.[37] These agreements tend to be used with highly secret projects or where commercially sensitive information is being shared with you, as an external consultant.

Many appointments also include confidentiality clauses – a combination of a cultural lack of trust and an assumption that others will steal your ideas, documents or information.

As documents can be emailed simply, or added to project databases, more and more information is being shared on each construction project – some of which should be kept secret and not disclosed. At the same time, trust between clients and consultants has eroded. This has led to an increase in the use of confidentiality agreements and clauses without any clear aim, reason or benefit.

## Avoiding Common Errors

Your appointment should:

- narrowly define information that must be treated as confidential, excluding information from other people or already within your knowledge; a wide definition can make it impractical to provide the services
- explain what uses are permitted; e.g. sharing with external assistants, funders, regulatory authorities, etc.
- confirm that the obligation of confidentiality no longer applies once the information is in the public domain (as long as it was not disclosed by a breach of the duty) or there is a legal obligation to disclose it
- confirm when the duty ends.

## Does It Really Matter?

### Rivals In Racing

In a 20-year development agreement worth nearly €¼m each month, Aerolab agreed to carry out aerodynamic testing of Formula 1 cars that Force India had designed and built. An express clause included a wide definition of confidential information and a duty for that information to be kept confidential except exclusively for services provided under the development agreement.

**Information or Expertise**

Certain data was copied after termination of that contract and used when working with a competitor. The issue which taxed the court was how to distinguish between confidential information contained in files and expertise gained in providing those services.

The court said it was clear *that the parties carefully balanced their respective rights and obligations under [the confidentiality clause] ... [and] the court should be very slow to substitute its own perception of what is reasonable for that of the parties to the contract.*[38]

The court decided that Aerolab had not misused confidential information either under the terms of the contract or as a springboard to gain an unfair head start.[39]

**Do You Need To Include Confidentiality?** No. There is an implied duty to keep information confidential.[40] The information protected is information which is important, valuable to someone, not available publicly, and distinguishable from generally available information. This includes sensitive information about a company's financial affairs, proposals for new projects, client lists, or costs from tenders. Whereas copyright only applies to durable media, confidentiality can also apply to discussions and verbal information.

A simple test to apply is to decide whether, if the information were released, it would harm the owner or benefit its competitors. There are some grey areas where it is hard to tell what the effect of disclosure would be.

Under common law, the duty of confidentiality applies until the information is no longer confidential. Essentially, your information is kept private until you choose to release it, which could be indefinitely.

You need to be careful what information you share with your prospective clients, but not simply because of confidentiality considerations. Under the Consumer Rights Act 2015, if you provide information to a consumer client – whether spoken or written –

about your business, your service or standards then it can be contractually binding. So what you say 'in confidence' can become a term of your appointment.

**Why Should You Keep It Simple?** Although you can prevent proposed or further disclosure of confidential information through an injunction, or claim damages for breach of the duty of confidentiality, it is far better to stop your client from publishing that information.

Certainty requires you to clarify the precise acts you want to prohibit and the information that should be kept secret. The simplest way of doing this is to make sure that both parties to your appointment understand that some information should never be shared, except where strictly necessary to complete the project or provide the services.

Confidentiality is core to building trust with your client and demonstrating your professionalism. If you cannot be trusted with her information, can you really be trusted with her project and her money?

**How You Can Write It Simply:** With consumer clients, it is rare for truly secret information to be shared and this simple statement will suffice: *The parties will keep information relating to the Project, Client or Services confidential except where required by law, the Project or where publicly known.*

With business clients there may be more at stake and your appointment should define confidential information and confirm the duty and its exceptions (although it will wreck your word limit):

> Confidential Information means all information designated as confidential by either party in writing or that ought to be considered as confidential including <specify particular documents or types>.
>
> Each party agrees that it will treat all Confidential Information belonging to the other party as confidential, safeguard it accordingly and only use Confidential Information for the purposes of this appointment or the Project.

This restriction does not apply to information that is publicly known, which was already in the recipient's possession, was received from a third party, independently developed or must be disclosed by law.

# 14

# RIGHTS TO CANCEL

There are three aspects to cancellation that your appointment needs to consider:

- A Cooling-off Period [Glossary] for consumer contracts during which your client can cancel your appointment without owing you any money and where you have to refund any fees already paid (this must be at least 14 days but can be longer).
- A right for your client to change her mind either before you have started to provide your services or afterwards, provided she pays compensation such as a cancellation charge.
- A right for both parties to cancel future obligations under the appointment for breach of its terms, known as termination. [Chapter 20]

## Avoiding Common Errors

If your client is a consumer, then your appointment must include a right for your client to cancel your appointment for a short, cooling-off period.

However, your client may believe she has a right to cancel your appointment for other reasons – such as the project has gone over budget, she has lost faith in your competence, she has lost her funding, she has got a better offer from another consultant, or something else.

This is not how appointments are meant to work. As legally-binding documents they create rights and obligations on both sides. Your appointment grants you the right to provide all the services and requires your client to pay for them.

In practice, it would be stubborn and pig-headed to use your appointment to force your client to continue to work with you on a project she cannot afford or no longer wants. The flip side is that you do not want to encourage your client to treat your appointment lightly and to enter into it frivolously knowing there is a free 'get out of jail' card. If she is going to have the right to end your appointment early without cause, then she should have to pay for that privilege.

## Does It Really Matter?

### Calling It A Day: Does It Have To Be Reasonable?

In a long-term agreement with a Housing Association for the provision of works and services, a consultant agreed to a term allowing cancellation without a good reason, also called 'termination for convenience'. The appointment also included a requirement for the parties to work together in *a spirit of trust, fairness and mutual co-operation*.

Following a review of the payments made, the Housing Association decided to cancel the contract as the appointment allowed, by giving the consultant 3-months' notice. The consultant claimed compensation for future lost profits, totalling over £1m. The court held that the appointment allowed either side to *terminate for any or even no reason*. The court said that the right to cancel the appointment was not a discretionary decision; if it had been then the right would have to be exercised reasonably.[41]

If the client's cancellation had to be reasonable then, based on principles in another case[42], the client would have acted unreasonably and in breach of the appointment if it had used the right to cancel as part of an ulterior motive such as harassing or annoying the consultant.

# COOLING OFF

**Do You Need To Include A Cooling-off Period?** For a consumer client, you must allow your client to cancel your appointment within 14 days (unless the appointment is made on your premises). Your appointment should also include a cancellation form, although your client is not obliged to use it.

The impact of these rules is that you should not start to provide the services before the end of the Cooling-off Period, unless your client specifically asks you to. If at her request you do provide services during this period, then either:

- your client can still cancel your appointment but has to pay for the value of any services provided
- your client cannot cancel if the services have already been provided in full before she decides to cancel.

If the services you are providing are low-value urgent repairs or maintenance then your client cannot cancel during the Cooling-off Period.

**Why Should You Keep It Simple?** If you do not include this right and relevant notice then you are not meeting your legal obligations under the Consumer Rights Act 2015.

**How You Can Write It Simply:** If your client is a consumer, it is critical for her right to cancel to be clear and simple. You can state:

> You can cancel this appointment up to 14 days after its date (not counting the date of this appointment). You must give notice in writing and send it to <name, address, email>, and you can use this form (although you don't have to).

**Cancellation Form**

To <insert consultant name, address and email>

The Client <insert name, address and contact details> gives notice that we are cancelling our appointment for <describe type of> services for the project <describe, including location>.

Date <insert>

# CHANGING HER MIND

**Do You Need To Include A Right To Change Her Mind?** No. Your appointment will still be legally binding and will entitle you to carry out all of the services.

**Why Should You Keep It Simple?** A right to cancel benefits your client, and helps build trust as it demonstrates that you recognise the collaborative nature of the appointment. Once it is clear that you cannot work together, you should make it easy for both of you to end the contractual relationship as painlessly as possible.

Any right to cancel due to a change of mind (termination for convenience) should reflect and allow you to be compensated for the profit you won't earn by carrying out the remainder of the services.

**How You Can Write It Simply:** The right to cancel should set out when your client can cancel and the monies payable. Your appointment could state *The Client may cancel Services due under this Appointment by <insert> days' written notice provided she pays for all Services provided and £<insert> to compensate the Consultant for its lost profit.*

When there are issues of fault or insolvency, then a better remedy for both parties is termination. [Chapter 20]

# PART D

# HOW YOU CAN WRITE EFFECTIVE STANDARD TERMS

So far this book has outlined the client-specific content in Part B as well as the more challenging aspects of a consultant appointment in Part C.

The alternatives you chose, or changes you make to your existing document, will depend on the needs of your business and your values. Both will affect the type of appointment you want to agree with clients.

To be truly effective your appointment requires a little more depth. It should:

- explain when your client can expect to start getting the benefit of your expertise [Chapter 15]
- ensure that the services that you perform are to the right standards [Chapter 16]
- minimise the risks associated with working with each other [Chapter 17]
- prevent those risks undermining your business' future and its profitability by limiting your liability [Chapter 18]
- be user-friendly by including procedures on payment and managing changes to the services [Chapter 19]
- set out some useful extra remedies in the event things do not go according to plan [Chapter 20] to help you avoid formal disputes.

This book guides you to what you really need to create a simple and effective appointment.

There are other 'boilerplate clauses' that your appointment could include such as the laws that will apply to your contract, currency issues, not acting in legal partnership and so on. For those clauses, you need to ask yourself: *If the clauses don't change my behaviour, build trust or help me avoid disputes, do I really need them?*[43]

# 15

# THE TIME TO ACT

As noted in Chapter 11, time is one of the three core expectations of a project. The relative importance of time depends on each project. You should ask your client which is her key objective: cost, time or quality?

For most appointments, your client is keen for you to start providing your services soon, but rarely needs you to *guarantee* that you will complete those services by a specific date. The duration of your services may, for example, depend on how long it takes to get approval from mortgage companies or planners, involve the supply chain or build the project.

Of course, if you structure your fees based on time spent (hourly, weekly or monthly), then how long your services will take is critical as your client will be financially interested.

## Avoiding Common Errors

Although a few standard appointments[44] include terms allowing extensions of the time estimated to complete the services, this is not really necessary if your services are well-defined.

Another mistake is to adopt legal jargon and make 'time of the essence'. This means if you are late your client can cancel or terminate the appointment, and she may refuse to pay for your services.[45]

Appointments can also state that they have retrospective effect. This is useful if you don't get around to your paperwork *before* you start providing your services.[46] However, it is far better to get the appointment agreed and then start work.

Your appointment should:

- include a *start date* for services, if you are not yet acting. Unless time is your client's key objective, your appointment does not need an *end date.*
- confirm if you are going to comply with any other specific client deadlines, such as applying for planning before an outline approval expires. The project programme does not need to be a contract document unless both you and your client need to be tied to fixed dates and fixed progress.

## Does It Really Matter?

### Take Your Time?

A dispute arose between the client (a design and build contractor) and its architect on a £20m project to construct new homes for service personnel. The contractor client sent all relevant programmes to the consultant. The contractor client claimed the consultant failed to provide design drawings on time (timeously), which in turn made the client late in completing the works.

The appointment *required the architect to ... provide designs in a timely manner to enable the contractor to meet [key dates under the building contract], provided that they are reasonable and achievable.*[47]

The court held that the parties *contracted on the basis that the [consultant] would perform its design services so as to enable [the contractor client] to carry out the contract programme.*

The court was also prepared to imply a term into the appointment to that effect, leaving the consultant liable for £800,000 damages for the knock-on effects of its delay on the contractor client.

**Do You Need To Include Time?** Time is not necessary for contractual certainty. Your appointment doesn't need to include (1) a start or a completion date (2) a period for paying invoices or (3) when instructions should be provided to create the certainty required for a contract.

If your appointment doesn't include a specific timescale for each task or obligation, each party is under an implied duty to complete their obligations within a 'reasonable time'.[48] It would be unusual to include a fixed date for you to complete all your services, especially if you are supervising the works.

What counts as a reasonable time depends *on the circumstances which actually exist*[49] excluding those under control of the party performing each obligation.[50] It requires you to neither act negligently nor unreasonably. It requires your client to pay you within a reasonable time[51] of receiving your invoices (unless a time is stated).

This vague requirement could allow you to be slow but steady, which may not be what your client wants. For example, there is no implied obligation on a consultant who is supervising the works to attend site regularly (only as required).[52]

**Why Should You Keep It Simple?** It is better to under-promise and over-deliver (i.e. be realistic and complete your services on time or early) than over-promise and under-deliver (i.e. make commitments you cannot keep).

Most clients – especially consumer clients – do not have projects that are date-critical, so your appointment can be flexible by requiring for you to complete the services within a reasonable time.

A few business clients do have specific time requirements, such as schools that require new buildings by the start of an academic year, or development projects which have to complete before planning permission expires. On these projects, you need to be clear what dates your client wants you to work towards, and check that they are realistic. Your appointment should not promise a timetable for the services that you have no hope of achieving or that is subject to matters outside your control.

**How You Can Write It Simply:** Depending on the extent of services you are going to provide, you can (1) adopt the implied term of completing within a reasonable time or (2) provide your client with an estimate of how long the services may take. You should not guarantee that you will comply with a project programme as some events are outside your control and the programme is often out-of-date.

Your appointment can simply say:

> The Consultant will provide the Services[, starting on <date>] and complete them within a reasonable time. The Consultant is not responsible for delays to the Services or the Project beyond its reasonable control or due to the Client's failure to provide instructions on time.
>
> OR
>
> The Consultant expects the Services to continue for at least <number> months and will continue to provide the Services until the Project is complete.

# 16

# THE STANDARDS YOUR CLIENT EXPECTS

As with time, quality is one of your client's three core expectations.

Many disputes with consultants focus on their failure to meet the standards their client expects. Are you promising to act professionally, competently or with specialist expertise? Are you guaranteeing or just trying hard to meet your client's expectations and objectives (whether explicit and implicit)?

To take just a few examples:

- Was the engineering consultant wrong in not telling his client that the contractor had not properly supported the basement works?
- Was the project manager wrong in allowing a contractor to continue to work on a large project, knowing that the building contract had not been signed?
- Was the contract administrator wrong to issue certificates when the works were substandard?

Meeting your client's expectations on quality or performance is a matter of competence and credibility (both essential elements of trust). No client wants to pay for the services of a reckless consultant!

## Avoiding Common Errors

Many appointments fall into the lazy option of adopting a low standard based on commonly used terms that the consultant will use 'reasonable skill and care' or will 'act professionally'. Some say nothing and hope your expertise 'goes without saying'.

However, if you really want your client to be confident in your skills, knowledge and experience (the reason she asked *you* to help her rather than someone else), you should clarify the standards your services will reach.

Your appointment should describe:

- The standards of performance for both you and your client
- Any specific outputs that your client wants you to achieve; e.g. to design a porch that cannot cost more than the client's budget. [Chapter 11]

Your appointment needs to distinguish between two measures for quality: an *input* measure (the level of expertise you should use) and an *output* measure (the extent to which the services meet the client's requirements). This is the difference between reasonable skill and care (input) and fitness for purpose (output).

Unless your appointment says so, you are not guaranteeing that any services you provide *will definitely achieve* your client's desired result(s).

### Does It Really Matter?

#### The Precise Performance Required

A contractor was appointed to design, manufacture, install, test and complete a project for 60 offshore wind turbine generators. The agreement required the designer to provide services to specific standards.

## Performance Standards

- with due care and diligence expected of appropriately qualified and experienced designers
- in a professional manner and in accordance with good industry practice
- so that each item of plant and the works will be fit for its purpose as stated in the specification, including a design life of 20 years.

The designer argued that the input (reasonable skill and care) and output (fit for purpose, 20-year design life) standards were incompatible. The court disagreed and held that the designer had 'warranted that the [works] could have a service life of 20 years' even though they failed in 2–3 years.[53]

**Do You Need To Include Quality Standards?** No. If your appointment is silent on quality standards it is still certain. Terms will be implied by legislation/cases that you will perform your services and your client will perform her obligations with reasonable skill and care.[54]

> *The law does not usually imply a warranty that [a consultant] will achieve the desired result, but only a term that he will use reasonable skill and care. The surgeon does not warrant that he will cure the patient. Nor does the solicitor warrant that he will win the case. But, when a dentist agrees to make a set of false teeth for a patient, there is an implied warranty that they will fit his gums ...*[55]

This is the bare minimum your client expects from her consultant. Reasonable skill and care simply means that you are 'reasonably competent', based on current industry standards, and that you will act in accordance with generally accepted industry practices.[56] Your client is probably hoping for a little more than Average Consultants LLP when she agrees to pay you a significant sum for your services. None of your marketing materials, website or proposals state that you should get to work on her project because you are merely competent (at least, I hope not!).

This is a more poetic explanation of your duty:

> *[The designer] must bring to any professional task he undertakes no less expertise, skill and care than any other ordinarily competent members of that profession would bring, but need bring no more. The standard is that of the reasonable average. The law does not require of a professional man that he be a paragon, combining the qualities of polymath and prophet.*[57]

**Why Should You Keep It Simple?** Clarity helps you to know with certainty the standards you are being asked to achieve and the expectations you need to meet to avoid claims for breach of your appointment.[58] You cannot hope to meet your client's expectations if your appointment doesn't mention them.

Keeping it simple at the start pays dividends well into the future. Your client will have chosen you as her preferred consultant based on her evaluation of your skills, knowledge and experience. She wants to be confident that you will meet any quality standards you said you could – that you are competent and credible.

**How You Can Write It Simply:** If your client wants the services to try to achieve a specific result or meet an aim, your appointment needs to state that result or aim. Your appointment should be precise, without *guaranteeing* that result or aim.

Your appointment can demonstrate your standards for your services by stating:

> The Consultant will use all the reasonable skill and care of an experienced <type of consultant> so that the Services meet the Client's expectations (above).

It should also contain a similar obligation on your client as this focuses her mind on her role:

> The Client will use reasonable skill and care in carrying out her obligations.

# 17

# THE RISKS YOUR APPOINTMENT MUST MANAGE

There is no such thing as a risk-free job or project.

Each site, each project and each client is unique. No-one can guarantee what will happen over the course of the next few months. Your client may change her mind about the services she needs, the project, the budget ... You may find that your beloved client won't pay, has run off with your design to a competitor, has submitted a bad review to a website, or simply won't answer your calls. She might even refuse to let you onto site. Every project involves taking a calculated risk.

Your appointment should help you manage those risks. Essentially you need to identify what risks may arise, how likely each risk is and its probable consequences, decide who should take responsibility for and manage each risk, and choose procedures to keep those risks under review.

Ideally, you should not start a project until the risks have been properly identified and analysed. Generally, the risks associated solely with your services are fewer than those on any related project. But managing risks for the project is important as your client may not want your services at all if there are too many risks; e.g. your analysis shows the project is not commercially viable or that her brief and budget will never match.

## Avoiding Common Errors

Your appointment should record who bears each identified risk and set out procedures for reviewing those risks as the project progresses. A fully comprehensive appointment would:

- state which risks are allocated to an insurer (e.g. breach of professional duties or design liability is often allocated to a professional indemnity insurer) or one of the parties (e.g. death or incapacity of a named consultant)
- include regular review procedures (e.g. for checking progress against your client's aims)
- demonstrate how the consequences of specific risks are shared (e.g. allowing you more time to complete the services, but not increasing your fees).

In practice, many appointments do not include a specific risk provision. As your appointment is for services which once provided cannot be taken back, there are two risks that it should address: the risk of not getting paid by your client (payment) and the risk of not getting on with your client (co-operation).

### Does It Really Matter?

#### Don't Be A Soft Target

How many times do you have to forgive your client for not paying you on time? There comes a time when you can refuse to continue to work with that client. The court agrees:

*Although this was not a contract of employment, the analogy is a close one. The judge found that the term as to the time for payment lay at the heart of the agreement. The breaches of this term were substantial, persistent and cynical. Not one payment was made in time; most were made inordinately late. These breaches occurred against a background of repeated complaints by [the consultant] and broken promises by the [client] ... The judge suspected that this was because [the consultant] was seen as a soft target.*[59]

## PAYMENT RISK

**Do You Need To Include Terms To Manage The Payment Risk?** No. Your appointment will still be certain enough for a contract.

Where your client is a business, you can rely on implied remedies such as recovering interest on overdue sums under the Late Payment of Commercial Debts (Interest) Act 1998, or suspension for non-payment under the Construction Acts 1996 and 2009. You may rely on a right to end your appointment for repeated non-payment as noted above.

**Why Should You Keep It Simple?** It is far better to deal proactively with potential payment issues. Simple terms will ensure that your client (especially one with little or no experience of working with a consultant) understands what she needs to pay and when, and focusses her mind on why it is important to pay on time. Implied terms, which – by their nature – are not written into your appointment, don't help your client understand her obligations.

If your client is a consumer, then your appointment should include an express term for interest on late payments, as the Late Payment Act does not apply. Having a *right* to claim interest if your client pays late is a useful 'lever' to encourage prompt settlement of invoices. You don't actually have to enforce it.

**How You Can Write It Simply:** Your appointment can state that:

> The Client will pay yearly simple interest at <insert>% above the current <Bank of England> base rate on all overdue sums.

## CO-OPERATION RISK

**Do You Need To Enforce Co-operation?** No. Your appointment will still be a contract. Every appointment includes an implied term that you and your client will work together, by:

- sharing information
- helping each other

- giving each other room to carry out your role
- neither preventing nor hindering the other (e.g. locking the site).

**Why Should You Keep It Simple?** Frankly, if you don't want to work together then you shouldn't be entering into any appointment. Making it clear from the start the behaviour you expect can tease out clients who disagree and may become troublesome. It also means your appointment is setting standards, managing expectations, acting as guide to good practice and helping you avoid disputes.

**How You Can Write It Simply:** Often the first step is to change how you view your appointment. Instead of labelling it 'terms and conditions', call it 'how we work together'. That improves the chance your client will read it and then use it. It encourages your client to see the project as a *joint* endeavour, rather than a chance for either of you to ride off on a whim of your own. You can set the scene at the beginning of your document by saying: *This appointment records the parties agreeing to work together on the Project.*

# 18

# THE LIMITS ON YOUR LIABILITY

There are two ways of limiting your liability for claims arising from your client's project. First, you can define and clarify the extent of your obligations, so your client really understands what you are responsible for. Secondly, you can add limits in time and/or money on your liability for breach of contract, to prevent you having to pay all the losses suffered by a disgruntled client.

Defining your maximum liability will help you reduce the risk to your business, may reduce your professional indemnity premiums, and can be factored into your fees. Your fees for any task will depend on a number of factors:

- the scope of your services [Chapter 9]
- your responsibility for each of the risks associated with your services [Chapter 17]
- your analysis of the potential impact if those risks occur, including failing to meet your client's aims. [Chapter 11]

## Avoiding Common Errors

The most common error is not recognising that a clear scope of services is the best means of defining your liability and excluding other liability. You can state what you are and are not doing to avoid your client harbouring any doubts.

Another failure in appointments is to include limits on the *consultant's liability* which are neither simple nor clear, such as:

- a compensation-sharing clause (a net contribution clause)[60]
- a clause excluding liability for indirect or consequential losses, which are either not defined or defined inaccurately
- a strict period for notifying or bringing claims
- an entire agreement or exclusive remedies clause which restricts rights and remedies to those expressly included in the appointment
- a clause requiring you to give a notice or invoice within a strict period if you want to charge for extras or get paid (a condition precedent).

If you and your client do not understand what these terms mean it can spell disaster. When reviewing a dispute relating to an appointment incorporating a net contribution clause the court said:

> *It is common ground that [the architect] took no steps to explain what this [net contribution clause] meant, if, indeed, he understood it himself.*[61]

If neither of you really knows what your limit is trying to achieve, you are not including terms which change behaviour, create trust or avoid disputes.

## Does It Really Matter?

### A Little Drafting For A Lot Of Court Time

A client sued his architect for £27m for failing to use reasonable skill and care in the design of a food factory.[62]

The court said that *it was common ground at the trial and in this appeal that [the architect] had a duty to consider, in relation to each*

> *of the rooms in which cooking was carried out, the risk that a fire might break out, the risk that the wall panelling might catch fire and, if it did, the risk of the spread of fire throughout the factory. It was apparent to everyone that the spread of fire throughout the factory could be catastrophic.*
>
> The architect's liability was in practice unlimited and the appointment could have significantly reduced the impact of this risk.

**Do You Need To Include Limits?** No. There is an implied *time* period for bringing claims for breach of your appointment, known as the limitation period. Simple contracts have a limitation period of 6 years after completion of the initial works, whereas deeds have an extended limitation period of 12 years.[63] [Glossary]

There are implied limits on the *amount* of any claim for breach of your appointment. The innocent party can claim the damages that would put it in the position it would have been in had the appointment been properly performed. It cannot recover losses which are not proven, are too remote from the breach, or are fanciful. But in practice the damages recoverable on a claim can be extensive: a consultant, who was in breach of its duties by failing to get the building contract concluded, was liable for the delay damages that would have been in the building contract.[64]

The other limit in your appointment is express – your *scope* of services. As discussed, it should clearly state those tasks, documents, consents, services or actions that are and those that are not your responsibility.

**Why Should You Keep It Simple?** Although all the terms in your appointment should be written clearly, there are three factors specific to limits of liability:

1 **Limits affect your reward.** You can take into account the impact of a simple limit on your liability when you set your fees. The higher the limit, the higher your potential risk, and the higher your fees need to be.

2 **Limits are closely scrutinised by the courts.** If there is any contradiction or ambiguity, the courts will interpret them against you.

3 **Limits are controlled by legislation.** For claims brought by a business client your limits have to be reasonable[65] and for claims brought by a consumer client, your limits have to be fair.[66] The wider and more complex your limit, the more likely the court will reject it as unreasonable.

**How You Can Write It Simply:** Rather than including a raft of different limits, you could simply limit your liability for any breach of contract claim, to a specific sum:

> If the Consultant breaches this appointment, its total liability for any one claim, excluding claims arising from death or personal injury, cannot exceed £<insert>.

The limit needs to be considered on a client-by-client basis and you should take into account:

- Your fees as well as the cost of the project
- The consequences for the project if you fail; e.g. if your design is defective, or if you fail to supervise an incompetent contractor, or if you instruct a contractor to proceed before getting planning approval
- The level of any relevant insurance that you maintain.[67]

Legislation means your limit must be at least your fees for consumer contracts.[68] English cases have upheld limits of 4–10 times the consultant's fees as reasonable. It is better to be generous and have a higher limit that protects your business, than aim low and have the courts reject your limit for being unfair or unreasonable.

# 19

# PROCEDURES HELP YOUR PROJECT RUN SMOOTHLY

Contracts are not just about what you are providing, but how you are going to work with your client. Your appointment should set out the process of getting from where your client is now to where she wants to be. That path may be obvious to you as an experienced consultant, but it probably won't be clear to your client.

Procedures deal with everything from payment, communicating information, project modelling, assisting each other, managing changes, to remedies when the project goes wrong including how you resolve disputes.

Most appointments implicitly rely on industry practices, professional processes and standard behaviours to supplement their express terms. The vast majority of procedures are not written out in full. Some may exist in internal handbooks, some are 'too obvious' to reduce to writing and others are unwritten rules of conduct.

## Avoiding Common Errors

Your appointment should strike a balance between including too many procedures (bamboozling your client and making it inflexible) and too few (making it useless as a guide). A sensible compromise is to include the processes essential to help you and your client work together. The key procedures are:

1. **Payment procedure:** required to build trust, avoid disputes and (for business clients) meet the requirements of the Construction Acts 1996 and 2009.
2. **Change procedure:** setting out how/whether the services can be extended or varied, including how the parties will agree the impact of that change on the fees being paid.
3. **Cancellation procedure:** agreeing when your client can change her mind about continuing and how much you would get paid. [Chapter 14]

## Does It Really Matter?

### Pragmatic And Practical

In an agreement between a consultant and an office provider, the agreement tried to control how that agreement could be varied. The agreement stated that *all variations to this [agreement] must be agreed, set out in writing and signed on behalf of both parties before they take effect.*

An oral agreement was allegedly made between the parties and a dispute arose on whether the clause prevented that oral agreement being effective. The basic principle is that the parties have freedom of contract and can waive any contract term which no longer suits their needs, against which the court had to balance the express requirement for *written* changes.

The court allowed the oral change saying:

*Those who make a contract, may unmake it. The clause which forbids a change, may be changed like any other. The prohibition of oral waiver, may itself be waived … What is excluded by one act, is restored by another. You may put it out by the door, it is back through the window. Whenever two [parties] contract, no limitation self-imposed can destroy their power to contract again …*[69]

### Is it also a contract?

The other issue for the court was whether there was consideration – one of the five legal essentials [Chapter 3]. The court said that the practical benefit of the change was enough to create value for the parties.[70]

## PAYMENT PROCEDURE

**Do You Need To Include A Payment Procedure?** No. However, if your client is a consumer and your fees are unclear or your payment terms are hidden, those terms could be deemed unfair and overturned.

If your client is a business, your appointment can either (a) meet the minimum requirements set out in the Construction Acts 1996 and 2009, or (b) rely on the payment terms implied into it by those Acts.

**Why Should You Keep It Simple?** Although you can rely on implied terms, the procedures may not be simple to read or simple to understand. In addition, procedures which are not written down are rarely used properly.

For a business client, it is just not realistic for your client to read four pieces of legislation to work out what notices she has to give and when, particularly when you can suspend if she fails to pay. [Chapter 10]

For a consumer client, simple payment procedures ensure your client will have the right budget available when you want to get paid, so she doesn't get any surprises.

**How You Can Write It Simply:** See Chapter 10 for a suggested payment procedure for your appointment.

## CHANGE PROCEDURE

**Do You Need To Include A Change Procedure?** No but it helps. In law, if your appointment does not include a change procedure (e.g. for changes to the services), then you and your client would need to create a new contract to cover the change. This can lead to confusion if there is an overlap or even conflict between the two agreements. It is also administratively more complex – the risk is that your client might not be bothered with the paperwork/negotiation involved and changes her mind ... losing you valuable work.

**Why Should You Keep It Simple?** It is inevitable that your client may *want* to change her mind, although she may not understand the consequences of her instructions. So your change procedure needs to be simple and easy to follow. If not, it won't be used and the new services may be instructed orally, leaving both of you wondering if that is a legally-binding agreement.

Changes may also affect the time your services will take (unless it is a like-for-like substitution) and the fees you want to charge. These should be agreed with your client before you carry out her instructions. She is entitled to the information she needs from you to choose between her original plan and her new plan.

**How You Can Write It Simply:** To protect your client's budget and to prevent your client overwhelming the scope of your current appointment, you could include a limit on the value of any changes. The procedure can be as simple as:

> The parties agree that the Services can only be decreased, extended or modified by written agreement detailing the changes to the Services, fees and time required, made before the Consultant starts to perform these changes. [The total changes should not increase the fees by more than <insert>%.]

# 20

# REMEDIES HELP YOU AVOID THE COURTS

Your appointment will create more trust and help you avoid formal disputes if it includes simple remedies when one party breaches its terms. Your appointment should take a pragmatic approach and include ways to help you resolve common issues quickly.

Under the Consumer Rights Act 2015, if your client is a consumer, your appointment should include:

- A remedy explaining how you will hear and resolve any complaints.
- A remedy allowing your client to ask you to re-do any tasks that she is not completely satisfied with or provide a partial refund.

## Avoiding Common Errors

The key remedy for appointments is termination. It is a serious step as it prevents you completing the services you are contracted to perform. It should only apply when your relationship with your client has broken down irrevocably. Termination should not be used frivolously or to put pressure on the other party.

Your appointment needs:

- a mutual right to terminate
- clarity around which trigger events will allow the parties to terminate
- a mechanism to notify the other party (written notice)
- a time period between the notice and when the services will end (best kept short)
- how outstanding payments will be dealt with.

Both parties should be allowed to terminate. Too often appointments only allow the paying party to bring it to an end. But if your client will not co-operate, will not pay, is preventing you from doing your job or goes bust, it is better to bring the appointment to an end. It would be a mere pretence to say that you are still working together ...

This Chapter focuses on statutory remedies and terminating your appointment.

## Does It Really Matter?

### When The Project Grinds To A Halt

After four months without pay, the architects on a large domestic refurbishment stopped work. They were finding it impossible to get paid and the project was grinding to a halt. The court said:

*I find that the [architects] were entitled to suspend work. They had carried out work in January, February, March and April on behalf of Mr Cunningham and Ms Good [the clients] and had provided invoices at the end of January, March and April in respect of the services that they had provided. Save for the single interim payment of £5,000, those invoices had not been paid.*[71]

### A most important term

On a completely separate claim for a remarkably similar project, the court held that the clients *were in breach of what to the claimant was a most important term of the contract, namely that reasonable sums due should be paid at reasonable intervals. Not only were the [clients] in breach of contract … for not paying, they were threatening (in breach of contract) not to pay any further sums until the works were completed … A refusal to honour payment obligations at least insofar as it relates to a relatively sizeable sum of money due or the threat not to pay further sums due in accordance with the contract must be capable of being [a breach allowing termination].*[72]

## STATUTORY REMEDIES

**Do You Need To Include Remedies?** No. There are four *implied* remedies:

1 Adjudication: most disputes can be referred to a swift dispute resolution procedure called adjudication (whether your client is a business[73] or a consumer).

2 Interest: if a business client does not pay your fees on time, your remedy is interest at 8% above the current base rate.[74] [Chapter 17]

3 Repeat performance: a consumer client is entitled to ask you to repeat your services if they do not meet the minimum criteria for time and quality or for a price reduction if that is impractical.[75]

4 Suspension: under a construction contract, if your client does not pay your invoices in full, and she has not issued a pay-less notice, you can suspend carrying out any or all of your services. [Chapter 10]

**Why Should You Keep It Simple?** Although these remedies are implied, not all of them are well-known, so it is wise to write the relevant ones into your appointment.

**How You Can Write It Simply:** For consumer clients, your appointment can provide:

> The Consultant will re-perform any Services which were unsatisfactory (performed late or without reasonable skill and care)

> without charge, within a reasonable time and without inconveniencing the Client. If repeat performance is not possible, the Consultant will refund <insert>% of the fees payable by the Client for that Service.

For business clients, your appointment can state:

> If the parties cannot resolve any disputes arising out of this appointment amicably then either party can refer the dispute to adjudication under the Scheme for Construction Contracts 1998 SI 649 (as amended), and the adjudicator nominating body will be <insert relevant body>.

## TERMINATION

**Do You Need To Include Termination?** No. There is an implied right to terminate future obligations under the appointment for fundamental breaches; i.e. acts which indicate your client no longer intends to comply with your appointment's terms. Insolvency will inevitably lead to such a breach but is treated separately in most appointments, allowing immediate termination.

**Why Should You Keep It Simple?** A simple right to terminate without the need to *prove* that your client has committed a fundamental breach may help you avoid legal proceedings. However, it is a legally complex area and by this time you may have fallen out, so there is plenty of scope for disagreement (possibly about whether the events constitute a 'serious' breach).

**How You Can Write It Simply:** Your remedy should leave neither party tempted to terminate for financial gain, but also neither worried about using the remedy when the circumstances are pointing inexorably to an irretrievable breakdown.

Your appointment could say:

> If there is a serious breach of this appointment either party may end this agreement by giving <14> days written notice to the other (or immediately for insolvency). After that period, the Consultant will not provide further Services, and will invoice the Client for a reasonable proportion of the next instalment of the fees to cover all Services provided.

# PART E

# NEXT STEPS FOR APPOINTMENT SUCCESS

Once you have actioned Parts B, C and D of this book, you should have an outline or draft appointment which meets the needs of a standard client, your business and the sort of projects your clients get involved with. It will be simple, robust and workable. You have also learnt how to plan a simple document that builds trust and avoids disputes.

You are now in control of your business, your services and your relationships with your clients.

Your outline 500-word appointment, by itself, is not enough to create success. You need to be able to create client-specific appointments that you and your client can read and understand. You both also need to be able to use your appointment properly. This means you need to:

- ask great questions to create your client-specific appointment [Chapter 21]
- after it is sent, focus on negotiating only the showstoppers [Chapter 22]
- after it is signed, use it effectively to continue to build trust and avoid disputes [Chapter 23]
- double-check you have understood all the guidance in this book [Chapter 24].

This Part will help you make appointments really work for you.

# 21

# CREATING A CLIENT-SPECIFIC APPOINTMENT

Although you now have the right outline content for your appointment, you need to learn to tailor it for each client. A one-size-fits-all approach does not work for creating appointments.

Your appointment should record your precise agreement with your client for her project. The quality of your first client draft is directly related to the quality of the questions you ask that client.

Each appointment needs to be different to the last, so you need to modify:

1. The name and details for your client, the precise services required, and the fees to be paid.
2. How you solve this client's needs and how your services meet her expectations. [Part B]
3. Copyright, cancellation and confidentiality terms – these issues pose different levels of challenge for different clients. [Part C]

If you really want your appointment to be client- and project-specific, you should carefully review every single one of your 'standard' paragraphs [Part D] before you send it to your potential client.

## The Questions You Should Ask

Before you send the appointment, ask yourself:

- What does your client *really* want to achieve (what does success look like)?
- Which of the key project aims (cost, time or quality) is the most important?
- Are there any other aims for this project that your client needs to achieve?
- How will your services help your client achieve her goals or solve her problems?
- What's special about your client and her project that you need to reflect in your appointment?
- Are there specific procedures or remedies that your appointment needs to include?
- Are there any specific risks that your appointment should help mitigate or manage?
- Does your appointment explain what's unique about your business and why that matters to your client?
- Does your appointment have your tone of voice?
- Does your appointment build trust?
- Will your client understand *why* they should work with you?
- Will your client know *how* to work with you?
- Will your client know *what* she has to do?

### Agree Before You Start Work

In a £40m claim relating to a defective car park, the consultants were arguing for a limit on their liability, despite having never signed a contract. The court said:

*I am conscious that, on my analysis, there is no limitation of [the consultant's] liability, despite the fact that every set of proposed terms and conditions included some sort of provision to that effect (albeit in radically different terms). Superficially, therefore, this might be regarded as a harsh result for [the consultant]. But on a proper analysis, I am bound to conclude that this was the inevitable consequence of [the consultant's] dilatory and often unco-operative approach to ... the negotiation of the terms and conditions. This case starkly demonstrates the commercial truism that it is usually better for a party to reach a full agreement (which in this case would almost certainly have included some sort of cap on their liability) through a process of negotiation and give-and-take, rather than to delay and then fail to reach any detailed agreement at all.*[76]

Once you have created a version of your appointment for your client, she will need to read it carefully to check that it accurately records her understanding of your agreement. She may want to negotiate specific aspects. This requires give-and-take as referred to above.

# 22

# NEGOTIATING YOUR APPOINTMENT

The purpose of creating an outline appointment is to decide, before you get stuck into a project, how you want to work with your ideal clients. It is far too easy to get drawn into tasks, discussions and negotiations, ending up with a deal which you would never have said *yes* to at the start.

The purpose of planning and crafting your appointment is to have a good starting point, which you then refine to meet the needs of individual clients. As discussed, it should be a fair and balanced document to build trust and avoid disputes. Your job is to avoid including showstoppers which I define as:

> *A clause or term that could bring negotiations or your appointment to a juddering halt.*

Not every client will accept your appointment without asking for some changes. This book has provided the background to the clauses so you have more confidence to stick to what's important to you (your showstoppers). Additionally, you should negotiate your appointment so that it suits both you and your client. You can create win-win agreements.

The key to negotiation is to know what you'd like in an ideal world and what you're prepared to concede. You need to decide your own showstoppers, but here are some changes your client may request that you should consider very carefully:

## Showstoppers

- Your client will not pay your fee until the related services are completed to her satisfaction. For most consultants, this could result in vexatious clients never paying a penny. If your client gets value, benefits or results from your services in instalments, you should get paid in instalments too.
- No limit on your liability, or – even worse – a clause under which you indemnify your client for any losses arising from your services relating to the project. You can't afford to surrender your practice for one client so always limit your liability.
- Your client having a right to cancel the appointment at any time without paying your fees to date or without compensating you for costs incurred or profit you won't make. This is a 'terminate for free' clause and is not advisable, except for the limited period (14 days) granted under consumer legislation.
- Your client asking you to sell or assign your copyright in documents, data or designs that you create. At most, your client needs an exclusive perpetual royalty-free licence.
- Your client having a right to deduct amounts from your fee without giving you a notice stating sound reasons.

## Learn to Compromise

For any term which is not a showstopper, and these are personal, you need to decide the limit of your ability or desire to compromise. For each client you must decide your 'walk away position' before you get too involved. That's part of being a professional and valuing your own expertise. You can get another client to help 'fill your fridge', but a bad appointment can leave you having to get another practice.

# 23

# USE YOUR APPOINTMENT EFFECTIVELY

There are a number of unhelpful myths about using appointments:

- You should not read an appointment all the way through – you should if you want to avoid betting your business on a roll of some weighted dice
- You should not query the terms in an appointment – you should unless the terms have been written so they cannot possibly be misunderstood
- You should not negotiate the terms of your appointment – you should as you need to work *with* your client
- You should not sign your appointment – although this is not strictly necessary [Chapter 3] it does ensure tidiness of process and prevents later arguments about whether it was actually agreed
- Once signed, you should shove your appointment in a drawer and never refer to it – you need to refer to it regularly unless you have a photographic memory for all the appointments you have agreed with all the clients you are working with at any particular time
- The only purposes of your appointment are firstly to get the job and lastly to resolve any disputes; so these are the only times

you need to read, understand and use it – no. Just no.

Your appointment can and should be a guide that explains how you will work to solve your client's problems. You cannot achieve success if you can't remember what you promised to do or how you said you would work together.

Your appointment legally obliges you to carry out your services and certain duties in a specific manner. It also sets out clear procedures to follow, many of which are linked to rights and remedies for you or your client. This is not mere 'dollying up' of what you always do. Your appointment is the critical tool you should employ to build trust and avoid disputes. Although trust is often built at the start by the use of a simple effective appointment, it is continued through following up on the promises you made in that appointment. You can hardly meet those promises if you can't remember what they are!

An effective appointment is one that the parties *do use*, which affects their behaviour, governs their conduct and controls their excesses. It can also nip disputes in the bud if you follow its procedures properly.

Please do not make the mistake of shoving your appointment in a drawer or allowing it to gather dust on a shelf.

Instead, as it is short and sweet, pin it to your noticeboard and keep referring back to it. Keep communicating with your client about progress to their goals and how you have met aspects of their expectations. Keep your client updated with any surprises (both nice and nasty) and be prepared to openly discuss any concerns she has as soon as they arise.

# 24

# MAKING SENSE OF IT ALL

When you have created your appointment, you might need to verify that you have understood and followed the guidelines offered in this book to ensure your appointment makes sense. Work through this Sense-Checklist, referring back to the appropriate chapter as needed

| **Is Your Appointment Client-Specific and Certain?** | Y/N | **Chapter** |
|---|---|---|
| Can you tell who the parties are? | | **8** |
| Do you understand precisely the scope of the services? | | **9** |
| Can you work out how much you are going to be paid and when? | | **10** |
| Can your client immediately work out how your services will meet her needs and expectations? | | **11** |
| Do you and your client understand your respective obligations? | | **8–11** |
| **Does Your Appointment Include Challenging Clauses?** | | |
| Can your client understand the limits on her use of your copyright material? | | **12** |
| Do you know which information is confidential or legally-binding? | | **13** |
| Does your client have clear rights to cancel? | | **14** |
| **Is Your Appointment Effective?** | | |
| Can you identify the start date for your services? | | **15** |
| Do you know the performance standard your client expects? | | **16** |
| Have you identified any relevant risks? | | **17** |

| **Is Your Appointment Effective? (continued)** | | |
|---|---|---|
| Does your appointment include a financial limit on your liability? | | **18** |
| Does your appointment include clear payment procedures? | | **19** |
| Does your appointment include a procedure for changing the services? | | **19** |
| Does your appointment include a right to terminate? | | **20** |
| **Will You Use Your Appointment Effectively?** | | |
| Have you created client-specific terms? | | **21** |
| Have you deleted or negotiated all showstoppers? | | **22** |
| Have you pinned your appointment to your noticeboard? | | **23** |

If you can say *Yes* to these questions then you are in the best possible position to use your 500-word appointment effectively and create project success.

Like all contracts, appointments are tools to help you do business. If you wouldn't use the wrong tool for a specific job at home, then you shouldn't use the wrong appointment to do a specific job on your client's project. An appointment should explain how your services meet your client's needs.

Rather than recycle any old mix of clauses, take the time now to create your perfect tool for that job: a simple, robust and 500-word appointment.

# GLOSSARY

| | |
|---|---|
| Cooling-off Period | Consumer contracts are required under English/Welsh law to include a minimum 14-day period during which the consumer client can cancel the contract without penalty. See The Consumer Contracts (Information, Cancellation and Additional Charges) Regulations 2013. This is also known as a cancellation period. |
| Simple Contract | Also known as a contract 'under hand'.<br>An agreement meeting the five legal requirements [Chapter 3] signed by authorised representatives of the listed parties. Contrast this with a deed. The limitation period for a simple contract is 6 years from completion of the last of the services. |
| Deed | A deed is a special form of contract. It must meet the five legal requirements for a contract and it must also (1) state that it is a deed somewhere in the document, (2) be signed as set out by law and (3) be delivered. The limitation period for a deed is 12 years from completion of the last of the services. |
| Fixed Price | Also colloquially known as lump sum.<br>In an appointment, a fixed price is where a price for the services is agreed in advance and this is the price that the client will pay, irrespective of how much it actually costs the consultant to carry out those services. The price can change if the services are varied. |
| Hourly Rate | In an appointment, an hourly rate is where each element of the services is given an hourly rate, which varies by staff expertise and not type of service. The price paid by the client depends on how long those elements of the services take to perform. |
| Payment Notice | A notice required under the Construction Acts 1996 and 2009. The notice can be given by either the client or the consultant, is dated and states the amount the party believes is due under the contract and the basis on which that figure is calculated. |
| Pay-Less Notice | A notice required under the Construction Acts 1996 and 2009. The notice has to be given by the client (as the paying party) to the contractor by a specific date. The notice has to state the amount the client intends to pay and the basis on which that new figure has been calculated. The Pay-Less Notice is required if the client wants to pay less than the amount on the Payment Notice. If it is not given, or not given on time, the consultant is entitled to be paid the full amount on the Payment Notice. |

# FOOTNOTES

1 Famously quoted by Donald Rumsfeld on 12 February 2002 in a White House briefing on weapons of mass destruction in Iraq.

2 A second version of this book will be prepared to cover readers from industries other than construction. Please email the author sarah@5000words.co.uk if you would be interested in learning when that book is published.

3 The definition is set out in the Construction Acts 1996 and 2009 (the Housing Grants, Construction and Regeneration Act 1996 and the Local Democracy, Economic Development and Construction Act 2009).

4 This applies if you are a trader; i.e. acting in the course of a business or trade (see s2(2)) and your client is acting outside the course of any business (see s2(3)).

5 http://www.therealestateconversation.com.au/news/2016/03/10/tenant-sneaks-cake-clause-lease-contract/1457564035

6 http://www.bit-tech.net/news/gaming/2010/04/15/gamestation-we-own-your-soul/

7 F-Secure included a Herod clause. https://www.theguardian.com/technology/ 2014/sep/29/londoners-wi-fi-security-herod-clause.

8 Even contracts of 50,000 words are the subject of disputes before the courts. The 2016 Nobel Prize for Economics went to economists who focussed on whether we should even try to create fully comprehensive (or complete) contracts. See Oliver Hart and Bengt Holmström: Contract Theory. Available from https://www.nobelprize.org/nobel_prizes/economic-sciences/laureates/ 2016/advanced-economicsciences2016.pdf.

9 Available from https://www.thenbs.com/knowledge/nbs-national-construction-contracts-and-law-survey-2015-finds-disputes-continue-to-blight-construction-industry included data from 981 respondents, of which 61% were consultants.

10 Definition from the American Plain Language Association.

11 The Consumer Contracts (Information, Cancellation and Additional Charges) Regulations 2013. Note that you should not start providing your services before the 14-day cancellation period has ended, unless your client specifically requests this. See Glossary.

12 Your trading name, geographical address and telephone number.

13 McGlinn v Waltham Contractors Ltd [2007] EWHC 149 (TCC), paragraphs 39 and 160.

14 In Globe Motors Inc v TRW Lucasvarity Electric Steering Ltd [2016] EWCA Civ 396 the Court of Appeal said that a clause requiring any variation to be in writing and signed did not prevent an oral variation of the contract binding the parties.

15 R Sikoryak created the iTunes terms and conditions as a graphic novel. Available from http://itunestandc.tumblr.com/.

16 More accurately, you can only contract with someone with the capacity to contract, which excludes minors (people under 18 years of age), with mental capacity (so excluding mentally ill people) and with companies acting within their powers.

17 Co-operative Group Ltd v John Allen Associates Ltd [2010] EWHC 2300 (TCC).

18 Schedules 1 and 2 of The Consumer Contracts (Information, Cancellation and Additional Charges) Regulations 2013.

19 This was changed by the Contracts (Rights of Third Parties) Act 1999 and third parties can sue if the party does or purports to confer a benefit on him or his class of people. In practice many contracts expressly state that no third parties can sue under this Act.

20 The 2013 Regulations require the geographical address at which the trader is established, the geographical address and identity of any person on whose behalf they are trading, and if different the geographical address of the trader's place of business.

21 Ampleforth Abbey Trust v Turner & Townsend Project Management Ltd [2012] EWHC 2137 (TCC), paragraphs 76 and 99.

22 Also known as quantum meruit, literally 'as much as is deserved'.

23 Footnote 9 above.

**24** The Consumer Rights Act 2015 requires the cost consumers pay to be tax inclusive.

**25** Cunningham & Ors v Collett & Farmer [2006] EWHC 1771 (TCC), paragraph 40.

**26** Section 15 of the Supply of Goods and Services Act 1982 as replaced by Section 51(2) of the Consumer Rights Act 2015 (for service contracts with consumers).

**27** Section 109(1) of the Housing Grants Construction and Regeneration Act 1996 (as amended). If your appointment does not contain an agreement to pay by instalments then the relevant provisions of the Scheme for Construction Contracts 1998 SI 649 (as amended) will apply.

**28** Where you are working on a monthly retainer then you can state: The Client will pay monthly fees of £<insert> starting on <date> and afterwards on the <5th> day of each month until <end date>. However, fixed monthly payments can result in queries about whether you are acting as an employee.

**29** West & Anor v Ian Finlay & Associates [2013] EWHC 868 (TCC).

**30** See www.gov.uk/copyright for more information.

**31** See Copyright Designs & Patents Act 1988.

**32** Fisher v Brooker & Ors [2009] UKHL 41, paragraph 29.

**33** Beck v Montana Constructions Pty Ltd [1964-5] NSWR 229. Cited in Blair v Osborne & Tomkins [1971] 2 QB 78 in which the court said for construction projects "when the owner of a building plot employs an architect to prepare plans for a house on that site, the architect impliedly promises that, in return for his fee, he will give a licence to the owner to use the plans for the building on that site. The copyright remains in the architect, so that he can stop anyone else copying his plans, or making a house from them; but he cannot stop the owner, who employed him, from doing work on that very site in accordance with the plans."

**34** Stovin-Bradford v Volpoint [1971] Ch 1007 which held that the implied licence extends no further that the minimum which is necessary to give business efficacy to the contract.

**35** In Meikle v Maufe [1941] 3 ALL ER144 the architect sued Heal's department store for using his designs for an extension.

**36** X Ltd. v Nowacki & Anor [2003] EWHC 1928 (Ch), paragraph 33.

**37** See https://www.gov.uk/government/publications/non-disclosure-agreements.

**38** Force India Formula One Team Ltd v Aerolab SRL & Anor [2013] EWCA Civ 780.

**39** Terrapin Limited v Builder's Supply Company (Hayes) Limited [1967] RPC 375

**40** A "duty of confidentiality that has been expressly assumed under contract carries more weight when balanced against the restriction of the right of freedom of expression than [an implied] duty of confidentiality": Campbell v Frisbee [2002] EWCA Civ 1374, [2003] ICR 141 at [22].

**41** TSG Building Services plc v South Anglia Housing Ltd [2013] EWHC 1151 (TCC).

**42** Reinwood Limited v L Brown and Sons [2008] UKHL 12 gives six principles to help assess whether a party has acted unreasonably or vexatiously in terminating or cancelling a contract.

**43** For an explanation of some of the more common boilerplate clauses, you can visit the Butler's Tale http://devant.co.uk/the-butlers-tale/.

**44** Notably IChemE Professional Services Contract, Short Form (2015) and the IEE/IMechE MF/4 A model form of Terms and Conditions of Engagement for home or overseas agreements for the provision of consultancy services by Engineering Consultants (2003).

**45** See Co-operative Group (CWS) Ltd (formerly Co-operative Wholesale Society Ltd) v International Computers Ltd [2003] EWHC 1 (TCC) where there was a dispute about whether the supplier had guaranteed delivery of software on a specific date.

**46** Trollope & Colls v Atomic Power Constructions [1963] 1 WLR 333.

**47** CFW Architects (A Firm) v Cowlin Construction Ltd [2006] EWHC 6 (TCC), paragraph 12.

**48** Section 14 of the Supply of Goods and Services Act (1982) as amended (for business clients) or Section 52(2) of the Consumer Rights Act 2015 (for consumer clients) requires services to be provided within a reasonable time.

**49** Hick v Raymond & Reid [1893] AC 22. Lord Watson said that a reasonable time "has invariably been held to mean that the party upon whom it is incumbent duly fulfils his obligation, notwithstanding protracted delay, so long as such delay is attributable to causes beyond his control, and he has neither acted negligently nor unreasonably." It is a question of fact.

**50** British Steel Corporation v Cleveland Bridge and Engineering Co Ltd [1984] 1 All ER 504.

**51** Which is longer than 2–3 days as contended for by Allridge (Builders) Ltd v Grandactual Ltd (1996) 55 Con LR 51. The court held it would be difficult to imply a term that payment must be made within two or three days of receipt of every invoice – the contractor was to pay what was properly due in respect of each invoice within a reasonable time of receipt.

**52** The frequency and duration of inspections required of a professional should be proportionate to the nature of the works going on at site from time to time, Corfield v Grant (1992) 29 Con LR 58 at 58–59.

**53** MT Højgaard A/S v E.On Climate and Renewables UK Robin Rigg East Ltd & Anor [2015] EWCA Civ 407.

**54** Section 13 of the Supply of Goods and Services Act (1982) as amended (for business clients) or Section 49(1) of the Consumer Rights Act 2015 (for consumer clients) require services to be provided with reasonable skill and care.

**55** Greaves & Co (Contractors) Ltd v Baynham Meikle and Partners, [1975] 3 All ER 99, Lord Denning MR.

**56** Bolam v Friern Hospital Management Committee [1957] 2 All ER 118.

**57** Bingham LJ, Eckersley v Binnie & Partners [1988] 18 Con LR 1.

**58** A failure to use reasonable skill and care is often incorrectly referred to as negligence. Negligence is the breach of the tortious duty to use reasonable care which applies whether or not you have a contract with that other person.

**59** Alan Auld Associates Ltd v Rick Pollard Associates & Anor [2008] EWCA Civ 655, paragraph 20.

**60** This clause means each responsible party only pays the share that is 'just and equitable' based on their responsibility for the losses suffered, and overturns the principle of joint and several liability. They are common across a range of construction contracts. For more information see my blogs www.500words.co.uk/blog.

**61** West & Anor v Ian Finlay & Associates (A Firm) [2013] EWHC 868 (TCC), paragraph 31.

**62** Sahib Foods Ltd v Paskin Kyriakides Sands (a firm) [2003] EWCA Civ 1832.

**63** Limitation Act 1980 ss5 and 8.

**64** Ampleforth, noted above.

**65** Section 2(2) Unfair Contract Terms Act 1977 for B2B.

**66** Fairness is based on considering whether a term causes a significant imbalance in the parties' rights and obligations, to the detriment of the consumer. Such terms will be deleted from your appointment and cannot bind a consumer client.

**67** Your insurance limit does not automatically limit your liability. See my blog http://500words.co.uk/insurance-or-limit-liability/.

**68** Under Section 49 of The Consumer Rights Act 2015, liability cannot be limited to less than the contract price.

**69** Alfred C Beatty v Guggenheim Exploration Company and others (1919) 225 NY 380 (New York Court of Appeals), Cardozo J (pages 387 to 388).

**70** MWB Business Exchange Centres Ltd v Rock Advertising Ltd (Rev 1) [2016] EWCA Civ 553.

**71** Cunningham & Ors v Collett & Farmer [2006] EWHC 1771 (TCC), paragraph 275.

**72** CJ Elvin Building Services Ltd v Noble & Anor [2003] EWHC 837 (TCC), paragraphs 90 and 91.

**73** Under the Housing Grants, Construction and Regeneration Act 1996 (as amended) and associated Schemes.

**74** As required by the Late Payment of Commercial Debts (Interest) Act 1998 (as amended).

**75** If repeating your performance of the service would cause you significant inconvenience or is impossible, then your client is entitled to claim a price reduction of up to 100% of your fees, payable within 14 days of agreeing the refund. See Section 56 of the Consumer Rights Act 2015.

**76** Arcadis Consulting (UK) Ltd v AMEC (BSC) Ltd [2016] EWHC 2509 (TCC).

# ABOUT THE AUTHOR

Sarah Fox has spent 20 years reading, analysing, critiquing, writing and training others on using construction contracts. At Eversheds LLP, she wrote, adapted, amended, negotiated and resolved disputes on contracts from 1 page to 100 pages.

She now specialises in helping construction professionals to build simple contracts. With JCT SB 2016 weighing in at over 50,000 words plus another 25,000 words of amendments, the simplicity of writing 500-word contracts has become Sarah's personal project.

Simple means readable, understandable and usable. 500 words is roughly a single A4-page. Her contracts are elegant, clear and brief, and – most importantly – legally robust.

With this book as your guide, you can create simple appointments. To get additional support, readers can sign up for Sarah's emailed regular contract tips and get access to a pdf version of the Sense-Checklist as well as a host of handy resources for consultants.

Sarah is an award-winning keynote speaker and is an expert in simplifying contracts and contracting, making your contracts easier to read, understand and use. Her first book in this series is *How to Write Simple and Effective Letters of Intent in Just 500 Words* and is available in paperback or kindle versions from Amazon.

**www.500words.co.uk**

**sarah@500words.co.uk**

# A THANK YOU CARD

Like being a parent or buying a house, you think that for the second one you have it sussed. Just like each child or house has its own unique anomalies and idiosyncrasies, the same is true of my second book. Many people have helped me along my 20+ year journey and here are some simple highlights ...

Thanks are due to my editor, Robert Watson, for checking clarity and crafting consistency and my designer, Andy Ashdown, for producing covers and layout that don't scream 'boring legal stuff'.

In just 12 months, my business mentor Steve Houghton-Burnett gave me the confidence to step into my own expertise and share that with others in my blog, speeches to international conferences, the media and now my books.

For anyone in one of my audiences who thought they were asking a silly question, thank you. I shamelessly plundered those angles to journey back to a time when I knew no law, to provide the guidance you need.

Lastly, to my three amazing sons who believed that writing books was the path to fame or wealth, and who are currently learning an important life lesson than neither of those are true.